LEARNING OBJECT ORIENTED PROGRAMMING THROUGH C++

A BEGINNER'S GUIDE FOR LEARNING OOP

DAVID LIVINGSTON J

ISBN 979-888546006-4

I dedicate this book titled "Learning Object Oriented Programming through C++" to God Almighty and His Son Jesus Christ. He is the author and finisher of our faith.

He gives knowledge and wisdom to those who ask Him. He wants to given us Knowledge, Wisdom and Understanding if only we ask. Let us ask Him and get the true Knowledge without measure. Amen!

The Promise given by Lord Jesus Christ

Contents

Foreword

This Book titled "Learning Object Oriented Programming through C++" is a practical guide for learning the fundamental concepts of OOP as well as C++. It introduces the concepts of Object Oriented Programming first. Then it introduces the fundamental programming elements of C++.

After the introduction to OOP & C++, it explains the topics related to OOP in C++ that include: Classes and Objects, Function Overload and Operator Overloading, Inheritance, Virtual Functions, Input Output Handling, File Handling and Exception Handling.

SECTION I - Basics of OOP & C++

The programming paradigm where everything is represented as an object is known as truly object-oriented programming language. Object Oriented Programming is a paradigm that provides many concepts such as inheritance, data binding, polymorphism etc.

The major purpose of C++ programming is to introduce the concept of Object Orientation to C programming language. In this section, an introduction has been given to both Object Oriented Programming and C++.

Topics covered in Section I are as follows:

- Introduction to Object Oriented Programming
- Object Oriented Concepts
- Introduction to C++
- Operators and Expressions in C++
- Assignment and Special Operators in C++
- Using Character Strings & Pointers in C++
- Defining User Defined Functions in C++

CHAPTER ONE

Introduction to Object Oriented Programming

Software development is a process of creating new software or modifying existing software that will meet the current requirements of its users. This process consists of various stages or phases in it. They are:

- Problem Definition (Analysis)
- Program Design
- Coding / Implementation
- Testing and
- Maintenance

A complete set of all these activities involved in developing software is known as Software Development Life Cycle (SDLC). This is because the same sequence of steps are to be followed whenever we develop new software from scratch or modifying existing software for up gradation.

Some small programs like text editor (e.g., Notepad) can be coded directly without following all the steps involved in SDLC. But, large programs like MS Word or MS Excel involve complexity in areas like understanding the problem domain, meeting the customer needs and delivering a good quality product in time.

To overcome the complexities involved in software development, many methodologies, tools and techniques were introduced. Following are two major methodologies introduced for simplifying software development process:

1. Structured (Procedural) Programming
2. Object Oriented Programming (OOP)

Structured Programming:

In structured programming model, software designers tend to use Top-Down approach, in which the overall objective of the system is defined first. Then the system is divided into various sub tasks or sub modules. With this methodology, software development is done by writing a set of sub programs, called functions that can be integrated together to form a complex system.

In Structured programming, the primary focus is on functions. A function is a sub program that performs a specific task using the values given to it through input variables (called parameters) and then returns the result to its calling program. Each function consists of a set of program statements and some local variables. A typical program structure for structured approach is shown below:

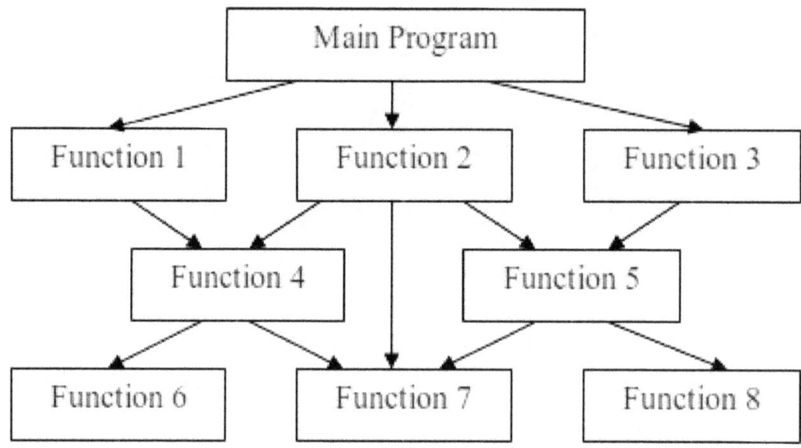

Fig. 1.1: Typical structure of Structure (Procedure) Oriented programs

A function when invoked behaves as though its code is inserted at the point of its call. The communication between the caller (calling function) and the callee (called function) takes place through parameters.

At the time of function call, the control is transferred from the caller to the first statement of the callee. All the statements in the function body are executed and then the control is transferred back to the caller to resume the execution of other statements.

Some characteristics exhibited by Structured or Procedural-oriented approach are:

- Emphasis is on doing things (algorithms)
- Large programs are divided into smaller programs called functions.
- Most of the functions share global data.
- Data move openly around the system from function to function and
- Employs Top-down approach in program design

Limitations of Structured Programming:

Structured programming was a powerful tool that enabled programmers to write moderately complex programs fairly easily. However, as the programs grew larger, this approach failed to show the desired results in terms of bug-free, easy-to-maintain and reusability of programs.

In this approach, very little attention is given to data used by the function. And, in a multi-function program, many important data items are placed in the global scope, so that they may be accessed by all functions. But, this leads to the problem of accidental modification of data due to its access from various functions of the program. Hence, in a large program it is difficult to keep track of the data items having global scope.

Another series drawback with the procedural approach is that it does not model the real world entities to the elements in a program in a one-to-one manner. This is because the functions are action-oriented and they do not really correspond to the elements of the problem.

The following picture depicts the relationship of data and function in structured (or) procedural programming:

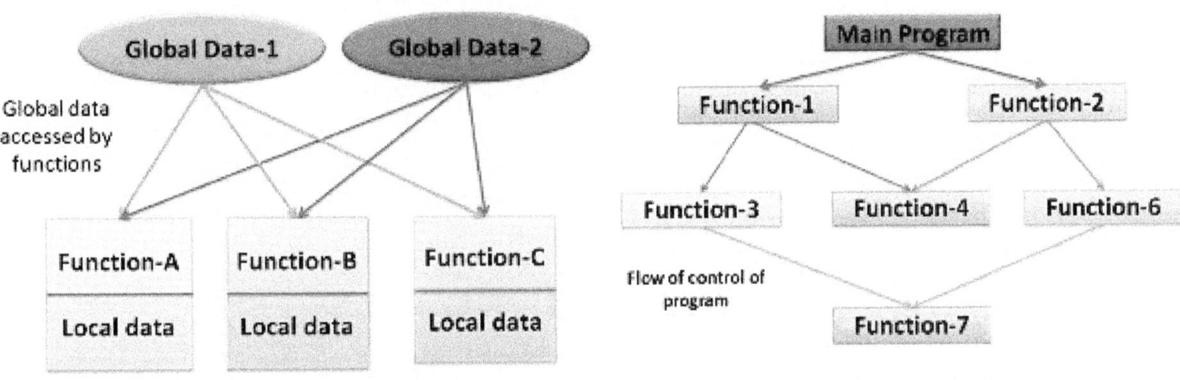

Fig. 1.2: Relationship of data and functions in Structured programming

Object Oriented Programming:

Object Oriented Programming is centered on new concepts such as objects, classes, polymorphism, and inheritance. OOP is defined as follows:

> "*It is a method of programming in which programs are organized as co-operative collections of objects, each of which represents an instance of some class and whose classes are all members of a hierarchy of classes united through the property called inheritance.*"

In this approach, any real world entity can be modeled as an object. The whole software is considered as a group of objects that work together to accomplish a particular task. During execution, objects interact with each other by sending messages and receiving responses.

For instance, in a program that performs withdrawal from an account, a customer object may send a withdraw message to a bank account object in order to perform a withdrawal operation. Any object that communicates with another object need not be aware of its internal workings but only its function signatures.

Object Oriented Methodology

OO languages combine both data and functions, the core elements of a program into a single entity called object. Objects allow localization of data and code and restrict other objects from referring to their local region.

OOP treats data as the critical element in a program and does not allow the data to flow freely around the system. It ties the data more closely to the functions that operate on them and protects them from accidental modifications from other parts of the program.

The protected data can be freely accessed only from the functions that are associated with them. However, the functions of one object can access the functions of another object. The following are some of the striking features of OOP:

- Emphasis is on data rather than procedure.
- Programs are divided into what are known as objects.
- Date and functions that operate on data are tied together into an entity called object.
- Data are hidden within the object and can't be directly accessed by external functions.

- New data and functions can be easily added whenever necessary and
- Follows bottom-up approach in program design.

The organization of data and functions in object-oriented programs is shown in the following figure:

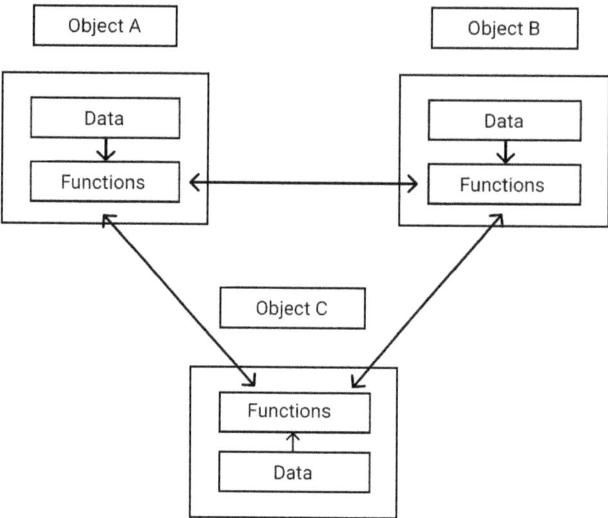

Fig. 1.3: Organization of data and functions in OOP

Consider an object - account with three attributes: AccountNumber, AccountType, Name and Balance, and three operations: Deposit, Withdraw, and Enquire.

In C++, objects are coded using a programming element called class. The following code illustrates this:

```
"class account {
  private:
  char Name[20];
  char AccountType;
  long int AccountName;
  float Balance;
  public:
  void Deposit();
  void Withdraw();
  void Enquire();
  }"
```

In this example, class is a keyword which indicates the beginning of a new class. The word account is the name of the class. The body of the class containing details about the data and functions of the account object and is enclosed with in a pair of curly braces.

The main advantage of using OO approach is reusability. Through this mechanism, an object already written can be reused to minimize the time and effort required to rewrite similar kind of objects. When a new object requires similar set of functionalities of an existing object and some additional features, instead of designing it from scratch, we can derive (create) it from an existing one.

CHAPTER TWO

Object Oriented Concepts

An object is an entity in a real-world problem. It may represent a person, a place, a bank account, a table of data or any other item in the real world. In software scenario, an object refers to a piece of software containing data and code that can be reused.

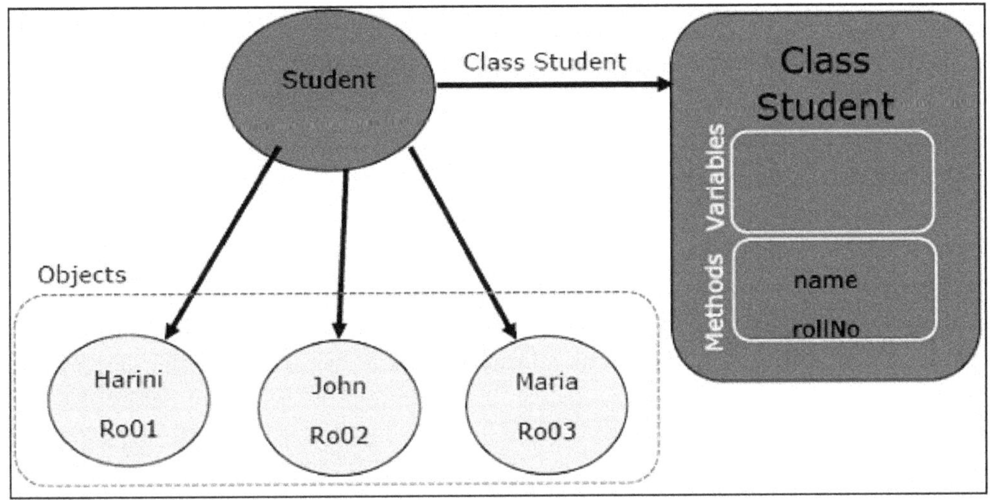

Fig. 2.1: Relationship between Class and Object

An object in a running program takes up space in memory and has an associated address to refer to it. Examples for objects used in a banking application are: "customer" and "account." During execution, objects interact with each other by sending messages and receiving responses.

Class & Object:

Class is a user-defined data type, which defines the structure of an object. Objects are variables or instances of type class. A class defines the type and scope of all its members.

There are two elements defined in a class. They are variables and functions. Variables declared in a class are called data members, and the functions defined in a class are known as member functions.

Every class describes possibly infinite set of individual objects; each object is said to be an instance of its class and each instance has its own value for each attribute. Following are the various definitions of 'class' data type:

1. A class is a template that unites data and operations.
2. A class is an abstraction of real world entities having similar properties.
3. A class identifies a set of similar objects.

Defining a member function:

A member function is a function, which is declared and defined for a class. Generally, member functions are declared within the class and defined outside the class. The function definition consists of two sections: a header and a body. The header part defines the signature of the function. It includes return type, name of the function and a set of parameters (variables used for passing information) with their type defined.

The function body contains the code that implements the function. This part can be written either inside or outside the class. To define the function outside the class, use the class name and the scope resolution operator (::) as a prefix to the function name.

Three types of scope specifiers are available for defining the scope of the members in a class. They are: private, protected and public. The scope specifier defines the availability of a member to the outside world. When not specified, the default scope of the members is private.

The private members are available only within the class. Normally, the data members that are hidden from outside access are declared as private variables. But, the member functions are declared under public scope, because they are free to access from other parts of the program. As member functions are the only way to access the private data and functions provided in an object, they are known as 'interfaces' to the object.

Encapsulation & Data Hiding:

The wrapping up of data and functions into a single unit (called class) is known as encapsulation. Though a class contains both data and functions, only the functions are available to the public, but not the data. The encapsulated data within the class are not accessible from outside world directly.

The hidden data can be accessed only through the member functions, which act as interfaces between the data and the external program. By declaring variables as private members, we can hide the data of an object. Variables declared as protected also implement data hiding. Such an act of hiding the data from public access is also referred to as data abstraction.

Abstraction of Function definition:

Abstraction refers to the act of representing essential features without exposing the background details required for implementing them. Like data, functions are also abstracted form the user by not showing the details of implementation.

Abstraction of function definition is done by hiding the details like logic and statements used for implementing the services provided by the object. In order to avail the services exposed by an object, the user has to know only the way of accessing the function and not the procedure used to implement it.

Polymorphism:

Polymorphism means having one name but different forms. Polymorphism allows two member functions of a same class to have the same name, but different parameters or return type. There are two types of polymorphism: Compile-time polymorphism and Run-time polymorphism.

Function overloading is an example for compile-time polymorphism. Two functions are said to be overloaded when they have the same name but different number/type of parameters or return type. Because the selection of an overloaded function is determined at compile time by the compiler depending on the parameter passed during function call.

Run-time polymorphism occurs during the function call of an over-ridden function. When a function of a base class (a class used for defining another class) is redefined in its derived class (class newly created from an existing one), it can have the same name, the same set of parameters and the return type as that of the base class function, but different body. In such a case, the selection of the function (function of the base class or the derived class) to be executed will be determined at run-time by the compiler.

Inheritance:

If we want to model an object whose functionality is basically similar to that of another object, then the new object can derive its basic functionalities from an already existing object. For example, the object 'plastic chair' inherits all the basic qualities like arms, legs and seat from an idol chair in addition to the extra qualification "material used" for making it.

Inheritance is a concept of OOP that defines the mechanism for creating a new class from an existing class called base class. The base class can be added on or altered to create the new class called derived class. In this way, a hierarchy of related classes can be created and reused in an object oriented programming.

Merits of OO Methodology

Object-oriented design involves identification and implementation of different classes of objects and their behavior in a real world problem. The objects in a software system closely correspond and relate to the objects in the real world in a one-to-one manner. Thus, it is easier to design and implement a system consisting of objects.

OOP languages provide a programmer the ability to create modular and reusable code using which formulating a new program can be done easily by composition and modification of some existing modules. The co-operation among different objects is achieved through exchange of messages.

Merits:

Since the objects are autonomous entities and share their responsibilities only by executing methods relevant to the received messages, each object lends itself to greater modularity. Flexibility is also gained by being able to change or replace modules without disturbing other parts of the code. Moreover, the independence of each object eases development and maintenance of the program. The following are some of the merits of Object Oriented methodology:

- Information hiding and data abstraction increase reliability and help decouple the procedural and representational specification from its implementation.
- Dynamic binding increases flexibility by permitting the addition of new classes of objects without having to modify the existing code.
- Inheritance coupled with dynamic binding enhances the reusability of code, thus increasing the productivity of a programmer.
- Many OO languages provide a standard class library that can be extended (extend ability) by the users, thus saving a lot of coding and debugging effort.

The advantages of object orientation also includes: shorter development time, high degree of code sharing and malleability (can be molded to any shape).

Demerits:

The runtime cost of dynamic binding mechanism is the major disadvantage of object-oriented languages. The following were the demerits of adopting object-orientation in software development in the early days of computing (some remain forever):

- Compile time and Run time overhead
- Re-orientation of software developer to object-orientated thinking
- Requires the master over the following areas:
    - Software Engineering
    - Programming Methodologies
- Benefits only in long run while managing large software projects, at least moderately large ones.

CHAPTER THREE

Introduction to C++

C++ is an Object Oriented Programming language. Initially named "C with classes", C++ was developed by Bjarne Stroustrup at AT & T Bell laboratories in Murray Hill, New Jersey, U.S.A., in the year 1980. C++ is an extension of C with a major addition of 'class' construct – a feature of Simula67 language.

Since the class was a major addition to the original C language, Stroustrup called the new language 'C with classes." However, later in 1983, the name was changed to C++. The idea of C++ comes from the C increment operator ++, thereby suggesting that C++ is an augmented (incremented) version of C.

Fig. 3.1: C++ - An Object Oriented Programming Language

C++ language corrects most of the deficiencies of C by offering improved compile-time type checking and support for modular and object-oriented programming. The ultimate goal of C++ is to provide a language for the professional programmer that can be used to develop OOP software without sacrificing Cs efficiency or portability.

C++ is a superset of C. Most of what we already know about C applies to C++ also. Therefore, all C programs are also C++ programs. The Object Oriented features in C++ allows programmers to build large programs with clarity, extensibility and easy of maintenance.

Fundamental elements of C++:

Character sets are the basic building blocks of any programming language. In C++, the character set consists of upper and lower case alphabets, digits, special characters and white spaces. The alphabets and digits constitute the alphanumeric set.

The smallest individual units in a program are known as tokens. Tokens are formed using one or more characters from the character set. C++ has the following tokens:

- Keywords
- Identifiers
- Constants
- Operators

- Terminals

A C++ program is written using one or more tokens, white spaces, and the syntax of the language. As mentioned earlier, C++ is a superset of C and therefore most constructs of C are legal in C++, with their meaning unchanged.

Keywords:

Keywords are special words, which are predefined in a language for a specific purpose in a program. They are explicitly reserved identifiers that can't be used as names for the program variables or other user-defined programming elements. Some of the keywords which are newly introduced in C++ are as follows:

Keywords	Purpose
int, float, double, char	Primitive data types
class, new, delete	Object creation / deletion
private, public, protected	Scope specifiers in a class
friend, inline, virtual	Qualifier for member functions
throw, try, catch	Exception handling keywords
for, do, while, switch	Control structure keywords

Fig. 3.2: List of Keywords and their Usage in C++

Identifiers:

Identifiers are names given by the user for the programming elements such as variables, symbolic constants, functions, arrays and classes. Each language has its own rules for naming these identifiers. The following points must be noted while forming an identifier in C++:

1. Identifiers are formed using alphabets, digits and underscore characters.
2. Every identifier must begin with an alphabet or underscore character.
3. The maximum number of characters used for forming an identifier must not exceed 31.

Since C++ is a case-sensitive language, same name with different cases are not equal. For instance, names such as rate, Rate, and RATE are treated as different identifiers.

It is a general practice to use lower and mixed case letters for identifiers. But keywords are always in lowercase letters.

Constants:

Constants are values that never change during the execution of a program. For instance, the value 10 is an integer constant, 'A' is a character constant and "C++ Programming" is a string constant. When such constants are named using identifiers, they become Symbolic Constants.

Symbolic constants are named constants that can be referred later in a program using the symbol used for their definition. There are two ways of creating symbolic constants in C++:

1. Using the qualifier const.
2. Defining a set of integer constants using the keyword enum.

Any value declared as const can't be modified by the program in any way. Consider the following constant declaration in C++:

"*const int size = 10;*
char name[size];"

The above lines of code declare a symbolic constant size with value 10, which is referred in the second line for array declaration using the name size. The default data type for constants is integer (int). For e.g.,

const size = 10;

means

const int size = 10;

The named constants are just like variables except that their values can't be changed.

Another method of naming integer constant is as follows:

"*enum{x, y, z);*"

This defines x, y and z as integer constants with values 0, 1 and 2 respectively. This is equivalent to:

"*const x = 0;*
const y = 1;
const z = 2;"

We can also assign values to x, y and z explicitily:

enum {x=100, y=200, z=300}

Data Types in C++

Data types are keywords that specify three things about an identifier called variable. They are as follows:

1. Type of data to be stored in a variable
2. Size of memory location required for storing the data and
3. The range of values a variable can hold

Data types are used in a program to declare variables. By declaring variables, we determine the set of values a variable can represent and the various operations that can be performed on it. Following are the three major classifications of data types in C++:

- Primary (fundamental) data type
- Derived data types and
- User-defined data type

Variables:

A variable is an entity whose value can be changed during program execution and is known to a program by name. A variable can hold only one value at a time during program execution.

A variable must be declared first before using it in a program. By declaring a variable, we reserve memory required for data storage and associate the memory with a symbolic name. The syntax for defining variables is as follows:

Data type *VarName1, ... , VarNameN;*

where,the data type can be any primitive or user-defined data type such as int, float, double and so on

variable names can be any valid C++ identifier except reserved words.

Primitive Data Types:

C++ supports the following basic data types: char, int, float and double.

"***char*** *- a single byte that can hold one character*
int *- an integer*
float *- a single precision floating point number*
double *- a double precision floating point number*"

By using qualifiers such as long, short or unsigned, we can have additional data types with varying size and range of values. The qualifiers short and long can be applied to both integer and float data types as follows:

"***short int*** *- Integer represented by 16 bits irrespective of m/c types*
long int *- Integer represented by 32 bits irrespective of m/c types*
long double *- an extended precision floating point number*"

The qualifier unsigned can be used with data types: int and char, in order to increase their maximum range of values twice. The qualifier unsigned restricts the user from storing negative values in its variables by setting the minimum range to 0. Therefore, the range of values for unsigned variables is 0 to a maximum value, which varies from data type to data type.

Integer Data Type:

An integer is a whole number without any fraction. For instance, 100 is an integer that represents the age of a person. Every integer requires two bytes of memory location to store the range of values from -32768 to 32767. If we want to increase the range of values to be stored in an integer variable, we need to declare it as an unsigned integer using the qualifier 'unsigned' as prefix:

"*unsigned integer age;*"

The variable ***age*** of type unsigned integer can store only a positive number and in the range of 0 to 65355. Thus, an unsigned integer uses only 2 bytes of memory for its storage, whereas a long integer takes four bytes of memory to store a number in the range of -2,147,483,648 to 2,147,483,647. The following table lists out the range of values and bytes used with various types of integer:

Variable Type	Bytes Used	Range
short int	1	-128 to 127
unsigned short int	1	0 to 255
int	2	-32,768 to 32,767
unsigned int	2	0 to 65,535
long int	4	-2,147,483,648 to 2,147,483,647
unsigned long int	4	0 to 4,294,967,295
float	4	-3.4E-38 to 3.4E+38
double	8	-1.7E-308 to 1.7E+308

Fig. 3.3: Data types with bytes used and range

Real Data Type:

A real number is a number having two parts: integer part and decimal part. The integer part has a whole number, which is followed by dot and a fractional number. A fraction is a value which is less than 1.

A real number can be represented in fraction or using scientific notation. There are two fundamental data types in C++ for declaring variables that can hold real data: float and double. A variable declared as float is assigned four bytes of memory to store a real number.

To increase the range of values to be stored in a real variable, declare it using the data type double. A variable of type double will occupy eight bytes of memory to store more range of values than a floating point variable. The following are some of the examples for declaring variables using fundamental data types:

int age;
float amount;
double per_marks;

Character Data Type:

A character variable can hold a single character, using 8 bits of memory cells. A character is represented externally in a program as a symbol enclosed in a pair of single quotes. For instance,

“*char alpha = ‘R’;*”

assigns the label R to the variable alpha. Actually, characters are represented in memory by a number, called code (ASCII code). For example, the code for letter A is 65, for B is 66 and so on.

A string in C++ is a sequence of characters stored in consecutive memory locations followed by a null character. The null character is assigned the ASCII code 0 and is called end-of-string marker. In C++, string constants are enclosed in double quotes as follows:

“Hello, World!”

Enumerated Data Type

Enumerated data type is a user defined type, which specifies a finite set of named values called enumerated constants. Like characters, enumerated constants are assigned integer values for their internal storage. Following is an example for declaring enumerated data type with enumerated constants:

"*enum color{red, blue, green};*"

The above statement defines color as a new data type of type enum with values specified as red, blue and green. Each of these identifiers (called enumerated symbols) is assigned a constant like 0, 1 and 2 respectively.

After the declaration, the enumerated data type color can be used for declaring variables just like a fundamental data type. A variable of type color can have any one of three values (red, blue, and green) at any point of time. For example, the statement:

"*color c;*"

defines c of type color that can be assigned a value like this:

c = blue;

This statement assigns the integer constant 1 to c internally. Because, enumerated constants are replaced with their corresponding integer values for their internal storage. The integers are associated with their identifiers at the time of compilation. They are supplied either by the programmer or by the compiler. Consider the following example:

"*enum color{red=10, blue, green=30};*"

In this declaration, the identifier red is assigned with the integer 10, blue with the next consecutive integer 11, and green with 30. If the integer value is not given explicitly to the first enumerated constant, it is taken as 0. Now, the assignment statement:

c = green;

assigns the value 30 to c. Suppose, two enumerated constants are assigned with the same value as follows:

"*enum weather{hot, warm=0, cold, wet};*"

then the constants hot and warm can be interchangeably used in order to assign the value 0, because both of them are assigned the value 0.

Use only enumerated constants with enumerated variables. If we assign any other value other than the one specified in the declaration, the compiler will give a warning message in order to avoid any invalid assignment. Enumeration is a convenient way to associate constant integers with meaningful names. Using enumerated constants in a program makes it easier to read and change at a later date.

CHAPTER FOUR

Operators and Expressions

Operators are special characters, which instruct the compiler to perform certain operation on one or more operands. Operands are data items such as variables or literals that the operators act upon.

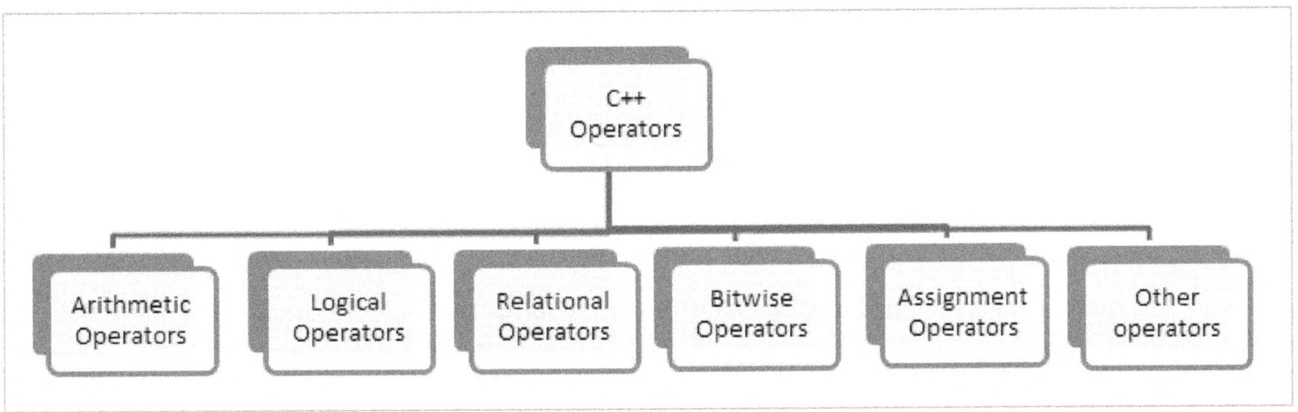

Fig. 4.1: Classification of Operators in C++

Some operators operate on a single operand and they are called unary operators. But, most operators require two operands to perform their operation and hence they are called binary operators. For example,

"*-5*
++i
--i "

are expressions that use unary operators, whereas

"*a+5* "

is an expression using the binary operator +.

C++ operators are classified into various categories based on their type of operation they perform. They are:

- Arithmetic operators
- Relational operators
- Logical operators
- Assignment operators
- Special operators

Expression:

An expression is a combination of variables, constants and operators written according to the syntax of the language. Every expression used in a program evaluates to a value. This means, after execution, it results in some value of a valid data type that can be assigned to a variable. The following are some of the valid expressions:

"*a+20*
*c+b*2*
total+20+c/3 "

The operands used in an expression may be of different data types. An expression with operands of different types is called mixed-mode expression. The following code illustrates this:

"*int a, c;*
float d, e;
e = (a+c+d); "

The above expression is a mixed-mode expression, which uses two integers and two floating-point variables.

Type Casting:

Mixed-mode expressions use type casting (conversion) for some of its operands before it takes on its final value. Generally, the operands of smaller size are converted to operands of larger size to get the right output. This process of converting the type of one operand to another is called casting, and is done implicitly by the compiler for mixed-mode expressions.

In an expression, for instance, if one operand is of type float and the other is of type int, then the variable of type int will be converted to floating-point type. And the result of this operation will also be of type float in order to accommodate the resultant value.

Arithmetic Operators

Arithmetic operators are operators that operate on numerical data and result in a numerical value. They take operands of type int, float or char. A character is also considered as an integer, if it is used in an expression, and the integer equivalent of the character (an ASCII value) will be used for its evaluation.

There are five arithmetic operators in C++. They are: + (addition), - (subtraction), * (multiplication), / (division) and % (modulo division). The operators + and – can act as unary as well as binary operators. When act on single operand, these operands specify the sign of the operand that follow them. The default sign for any number used in an expression is + (positive).

Among these two unary operators (+ and -), the negative sign (-) is used often. It is used to specify a negative number or to negate the value stored in a variable. For e.g., consider the following statements:

"*int x = 5;*
y = -x; "

These two lines of code assign the value 5 to x, and then negates. Therefore, the final value of y is -5. If x is assigned the value -5 (i.e., x = -5) in the above example, then the value of y will be 5.

Binary Arithmetic Operators:

The operators + and – take two operands if they are used for performing addition or subtraction on numbers. Depending on the type of operands they operate on, they perform either integer or floating-point arithmetic operation. When both operands are integer, then integer arithmetic is performed, which always yield an integer result. For instance, x and y are integers with values 16 and 5, the arithmetic is done like this:

"*int x = 16, y = 5;*
x + y = 21 and
x – y = 11 "

Not only + and -, but also other arithmetic operators operate on two operands. The multiplication operator (*) multiplies two numbers. The division operator (/) divides the first operand by the second operand and returns the quotient, whereas modulo division (%) is also a division operator except that it returns the remainder as its result.

Floating-point Arithmetic:

Floating-point arithmetic involves operands of type float or double with their values specified either in decimal or exponential notation. The result is also a floating-point number, but rounded off to the number of significant digits specified. All the binary operators except modulo division operate on floating point operands. The following statements illustrate the use of arithmetic operators:

"*flaot a = 14.0, b = 4.0;*
p = a / b;
q = b / a;
r = a + b; "

The above operations result in values 3.500000, 0.285714, and 18.00000 for p, q and r respectively.

Mixed-mode Arithmetic:

In mixed-mode arithmetic, if either one of the operands is real, the resultant value is always real. For e.g.,

35 / 5.0 = 7.0

Here, since 5.0 is a double constant, 35 is converted to a value of type double (35.0) and the result is also a double constant.

Precedence of Arithmetic Operators:

Precedence determines the order of evaluating operators in an expression. Generally, operators are evaluated from left to right in an expression. While evaluating an expression, the following rules of precedence are applied on operators:

- Operators within parenthesis are processed first. Within parenthesis operators are evaluated from left to right.
- Operators having higher priorities, which include *, / and % are applied next.
- Operators such as + and – (having lower priority) are applied last.

Hence, a complex expression formed using parenthesis and a set of arithmetic operators and operands may take two to three passes to complete the entire evaluation process. During the first pass, operators within the parenthesis are evaluated; then the operators with higher precedence and finally operators with lower precedence are processed.

Relational and Logical Operators

A relational operator is a kind of operator, which is used to make comparisons between two operands. All relational operators are binary operators and require two operands.

In a relational expression, the relational operator compares its left hand side operand with its right hand side operand. The result of this comparison will be an integer (zero or non-zero value). If the comparison evaluates to true, it is indicated by a non-zero value, otherwise 0 will be the result to indicate false. The following are the list of relational operators and their meaning:

Operator	Meaning
<	Less than
>	Greater than
<=	Less than or equal to
>=	Greater than or equal to
==	Equal to
!=	Not equal to

Fig. 4.2: Relational Operators in C++

Relational operators are used generally in a comparison statement like if... else in C. If the expression given in the conditional part of if statement evaluates to true, the statements written in if block executes, otherwise, the statements in the else part executes. The syntax of if... else statement is this:

"*if (condition)*
statement (s)
else
statement (s)"

In relational expressions, similar quantities are often compared for taking decisions. Based on the result of the expression evaluation, the control is transferred to execute the corresponding block of statement.

Logical Operators:

Logical operators are operators used for the following two purposes:

1. To combine two or more relational expression
2. To negate the result of a logical expression from true to false or vice versa

There are three logical operators provided in C++ for forming complex logical expressions. They are given in the following table:

Operator	Meaning
&&	Logical AND
||	Logical OR
!	Logical NOT

Fig. 4.3: Logical Operators in C++

The first two logical operators (&& and ||) are binary and are used to combine two or more logical condition, where as the third operator – exclamation (!) is a unary operator and is used to negate a condition.

The logical AND (&&) takes two expressions, one at its left and one at its right and checks whether both are evaluated to true. If both expressions evaluate to true, the result will be true (a non-zero value) or else false (0).

The logical OR (||) does the comparison of two expressions, one at its left, another at its right, to know whether one of the expressions evaluate to true. If either or both of them results in true, it evaluates to a non-zero value indicating true, or else false (0). The following table shows the various possibilities of condition 'a' and 'b' and the result of applying logical operators on them:

Operator 1 (a)	Operator 2 (b)	~a	~b	a && b	a || b
F	F	T	T	F	F
F	T	T	F	F	T
T	F	F	T	F	T
T	T	F	F	T	T

Fig. 4.4: Evaluating a Logical Expression having Logical Operators

Logical NOT:

The ! (NOT) operator takes a single expression and evaluates to true if the expression is false, and evaluates to false if the expression is true. In other words, it just reverses the value of the expression. For example, the expression

"*!(x >= y)* "

is evaluated as x < y. Similarly, the expression

"*a = = 0* "

is equivalent to !a. The expression !a evaluates to true if the variable a holds zero, false otherwise.

Logical Operator Precedence:

While evaluating the expression, the unary operator – negation (!) has the highest priority among the three, followed by the logical AND (&&) and then the logical OR (||). They are evaluated from left to right. The following program illustrates the use of logical expression to find whether a given year is leap or not:

```
#include <iostream.h>
void main()
{
int year;
cout << "Enter any year :";
cin >> year;
if( (year % 4 == 0 && year % 100 != 0) || (year % 400 == 0))
cout << year << "is a leap year";
else
cout << year << "is not a leap year";

}
```

Assignment Operator:

An assignment operator is an equal sign (=) which evaluates the expression on the right and assigns the resultant value to the variable on the left. Using this operator, we can do the following:

1. Initial values can be assigned to variables at the beginning of (a program) their usage in a program and
2. The result of an expression can be stored in a variable for later use.

The general form of the assignment statement is as follows:

"*variable-name = expression;* "

The expression can be a constant, variable name, or an expression (combination of variables, constants and operators). An example for an assignment statement is as follows:

a = c + d – 5;

CHAPTER FIVE

Assignment and Special Operators in C++

Combined assignment operator is an assignment operator which is prefixed by an arithmetic operator like +, -, * etc. The following is a list of possible compound assignment operators:

"+=, -=, /=, %=, &=, |=, <<=, >>="

Only binary operators can be combined with assignment operator to form a combined assignment operator. The syntax for compound assignment expression is as follows:

"*variable operator = expression / constant/ function;*"

These operators evaluate the expression on their right, and use the result to perform the corresponding operation on the variable on the left. Thus the statement:

"*variable operator = expression;*"

is equivalent to

"*variable = variable operator expression;*"

For example, the assignment statement

"*i += 10;*"

is evaluated as

i = i + 10;

Special Operators

C++ has a rich set of operators. All C operators are valid in C++ also. In addition, C++ introduces some more operators as given below:

Operator	Name
<<	Insertion operator
>>	Extraction operator
::	Scope Resolution operator
→*	Pointer-to-Member operator
::*	Pointer-to-Member operator
.*	Pointer-to-Member operator
delete	Memory release operator
new	Memory allocation operator
setw	Field Width operator

Fig. 5.1: Special Operators in C++

The operators << and >> are used along with cin and cout objects for performing stream I/O with console devices such as Keyboard and Monitor. Similarly the operators -endl and setw are used to format the data output with Console or File. These operators, also called manipulators, help the programmer to perform formatted I/O.

The pointer related operators of C++ are: -->, *, ::* and .*. They are used to access the members of a class (both data and member functions) through pointers. The operators new and delete are similar to the functions malloc() and free() in C. They perform the task of allocating and freeing the memory in a better and easier way.

New and Delete Operators:

Using new and delete can help us to allocate the memory dynamically (at runtime). This technique is required when it is not known in advance how much of memory is needed for a variable or object. Since these operators manipulate memory on the free store, they are also known as free store operators.

The new operator can be used to create objects of any type. The life time of an object created dynamically is directly under control and is unrelated to the block structure of the program. A data object created inside a block with new will remain in existence until it is explicitly destroyed by using delete.

The new keyword takes the following general form:

"*pinter-variable = new data-type;*"

Here, pointer-variable is a pointer of type data-type. The new operator allocates sufficient memory to hold a data object of type data-type and returns the address of the object, which will be stored in the pointer-variable. The data-type may be any valid data type. Consider the following example:

"*int *p = new int;*
*float *q = new float;*"

where, p and q are pointers of type int and float. They are used to point the memory locations allocated dynamically using new keyword and a corresponding data type. Subsequently, the statements:

> "**p = 25;*
> **q = 7.5;*"

Assign 25 to the newly created int object and 7.5 to the flaot object. The above two sets of statements used for declaring and assigning values to pointers can be combined into one set as follows:

> "*int *p = new int(25);*
> *float *q = new float(7.5);*"

When the data objects created dynamically are no longer needed, they can be destroyed using the delete keyword. Delete keyword releases the memory space allocated for an object so that the memory can be reused for another object.

The general form of delete operator is.

> "*delete pinter-variable;*"

The pointer-variable is a pointer that points to the data object created with new operator. Examples for using delete keyword are:

delete p, q;

Scope Resolution Operator (::)

Like C, C++ is a block-structured language. A block is a set of statements enclosed within curly braces { }. Block determines the scope of its variables that extend from the point of its declaration till the end of the block.

A variable declared inside a block is said to be local to that block. Consider the following segment of a program:

```
"..................
..................
{
int x = 10;
}
..................
..................
{
int x = 1;
}"
```

Here, two blocks are used and in each block, the variable x is declared and assigned with a different value. The value of x in the first block is 10, but it holds 1 in the second block. Statements in the first block can't refer to the variable x declared in the second block, and vice versa.

Blocks in C++ are often nested. Consider the following statement containing nested block:

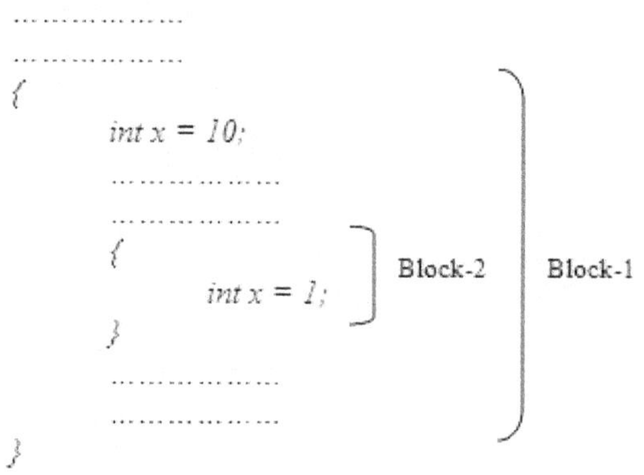

```
………………
………………
{
        int x = 10;
        ………………
        ………………
        {                              ]  Block-2        Block-1
                int x = 1;
        }
        ………………
        ………………
}
```

Fig. 5.3: Creating Blocks of Code in C++

In this program segment, we have two blocks: Block-1 and Block-2. The Block-2 is contained in Block-1, i.e., Block-1 is the outer block and Block-2 is the inner block. The variable x is declared both in the inner and the outer blocks.

The variable declaration of x in the inner block hides the declaration of the same variable in the outer block, and therefore, each declaration of x causes it to refer to a different data object. Within the inner block, the variable x will refer to the data object declared therein.

C++ resolves the problem of accessing hidden variable, i.e., accessing the outer block variable from the inner block, by introducing the operator ::, which is called scope resolution operator. Thus, the use of the scope resolution operator, in general, is to uncover the hidden variables. It takes the following form:

"*:: variable-name*"

The following example illustrates the use of this operator to access the global version of a variable:

```
"#include <iostream.h>
int n = 100;
main()
{
int i, n, a[::n];
cout<<"Enter the limit [0..100] :";
cin>>n;
cout<<"Enter "<<n<<"Numbers :";
for(i=0; i<n; i++)
cin>>a[i];
}"
```

In this example, we have two instances of variable n – the global one and a local one. The global variable n contains the value 100, whereas the value of the local variable n is given by the user. The global variable n is used for array declaration, but the local instance of n is for array manipulation (array storage and access).

A major application of the scope resolution operator is to separate the class declaration from its definition, i.e., to define a member function outside the class. Here, it is used to identify the class to which a member function belongs, when the member function is defined outside the class.

CHAPTER SIX

Character Strings & Points in C++

A Character String is a sequence of characters that are stored in consecutive memory locations followed by a null character (\0). The null character has an ASCII code 0 and is called the end-of-string marker in C++. For e.g., the string constant "C++ Programming" is stored in the memory as follows:

Fig. 6.1: Storing a string of Characters in an Array

Internally, each memory location of the above string holds an ASCII equivalent of the respective character. The null character (a byte with value zero) is placed at the end of the string.

String constants are always enclosed in double quotes as follows:

"Hello, World!"

String constants are useful while conveying some message to the user. For e.g., the statement

cout << "Enter an ASCII code (0 – 127):";

will display the string (Enter an ASCII code (0 – 127):) that follows the insertion operator (<<) on the screen. Strings are also used for storing and manipulating text such as words, names and sentences.

Declaring a String Variable:

A string variable is declared as one dimensional array of characters as follows:

"*char array-name[size];* "

where, size is an integer that specifies the length of the string. The maximum length of the string is always one less than the size (size-1), because one storage location must be reserved for storing the end of the string character. For instance,

"*char title[50];* "

declares an array named title with 50 memory locations. But, the maximum number of characters that can be stored in this array is 49, because of the reason that the last character should be an end-of-string character.

Another way of declaring a string is using character pointer. A pointer can be considered as an alternative to an array, because the name of the array itself is a pointer to the first location of the array. The following example illustrates this:

"*char * title;*

title = "C++ Programming"; "

The above lines of code will declare a pointer variable of type char that points to the string "C++ Programming", which is stored in memory using consecutive memory locations. The pointer title points at the first character of the string, and it reads up to the end of the string for retrieving the string.

The input and output operations with strings through pointers can be done as follows:

```
"char * title;
    cin<<title;
    cout>>title; "
```

When passing a string as a parameter to a function, it can be passed through a character pointer, but not using array name. Through the character pointer (parameter) the string can be accessed with in the function. The following example illustrates this:

```
class Person{
char name[30];
int age;
Public:
void getData(void);
void Display(void);
};
void Person::getData(void)
{
cout<< "Enter Name: ";
cin>>name;
cout<< "Enter Age: ";
cin>>age;
}
Void Person::Display()
{
cout<< "\n Name: "<<name;
cout<< "\n Age: "<<age;
}
void main(){
Person p;
p.getData();
p.Display();
}
```

Initializing a String:

Strings can be initialized at the time of its declaration using the following syntax:

"*char array-name[size] = {list of values separated by comma};* "

For instance, the statement:

char month[] = {'A', 'p', 'r', 'i', 'l', 0};

defines the string variable month and assigns to it the string "April.". The actual size of the string is 6. Because, the last character is 0 (zero), which indicates the end of the string and it occupies the last position of the character array.

The end-of-string can also be marked with the character '\0'.

The end-of-string character must be given explicitly when the initialization is done character by character. But, for a string constant, it is assigned implicitly as in the following statement:

char month[] = "April";

In this case, the compiler takes care of storing the ASCII codes of the characters of the string in memory, and it assigns the NULL character at the end.

Pointers in C++

A pointer is a variable used for storing the address of a memory location. Every pointer must be declared first before it is used in a program. This is due to the reason that a pointer can point only one type of data, just like a variable can hold only the data of a particular data type. For instance, consider the pointer declaration given below:

"*int* a;*"

This statement declares a as an integer pointer that can hold only the address of an integer. Similarly a pointer to a float variable can point only a memory location that holds a floating point number.

The main usage of pointers in an OOP language like C++ is to access the memory locations, which are allocated at run-time (i.e. dynamically). The process of allocating memory space for variables or objects during the course of program execution is called dynamic memory allocation. The other usages of pointers are as follows:

1. Accessing array elements
2. Passing the arguments to functions by address. This mechanism lets the modification of formal arguments reflect back on the actual arguments in the caller.
3. Passing arrays and strings to functions and
4. Creating data structures such as Linked List, Trees and Graphs.

Pointer Declaration and Initialization:

Specifying the data type for the pointer is the first step involved in declaring a pointer variable. Before its declaration, we should determine the type of variable a pointer would point to. The following is the syntax given for declaring a pointer variable:

"*Datatype * ptrVar1, ptrVar2, ... ptrVarn;*"

where,

DataType could be a primitive data type or user defined data type like Class or Structure

ptrVar1, ptrVar2, ptrVarn could be any valid C++ variable name.

In pointer declaration, the symbol * (called Asterisk) is used to inform the compiler that the variable declared (ptrVar) is a pointer variable. The pointer so created can hold the address of any variable of the specified type. Some typical pointer declarations are as follows:

"*int* pmarks;*
char name;*
Date pDate;*"

The first two declarations declare pointers of primitive data type, and hence the pointer pmarks can point only the variables of type integer and the variable name can point only a character. The third pointer variable is a pointer to a user-defined data type Date. Using it (pDate), we can point a date containing three fields: dd, mm and yy.

A pointer variable refers to a memory location, which contains the address of another memory location. Hence, after the declaration, a pointer must be assigned with an address of a memory location (or variable) so that it will point somewhere in memory. This can be implemented in code as follows:

```
"int marks, *pmarks;
  pmarks = &marks; "
```

In the above example, pmarks is a pointer variable of type integer and marks is an ordinary variable that can store an integer. After the declaration, the address of the variable marks is assigned to the pointer pmarks using the Address Opeartor (&) so that through pointer pmarks we can access the variable marks.

Dereferencing of Pointers:

Dereferencing is the process of accessing and manipulating the data stored in the memory location pointed by a pointer. This process can be done through the use of Dereferencing operator * (asterisk). The operator * is used for both dereferencing as well as declaration of pointers. Example code for pointer dereferencing is as follows:

```
"int *pmark, mark;
  pmark = &mark;
  *pmark = 100;
  cout<<*pmark; "
```

In this example, the pointer pmark points to the integer variable mark that will hold an integer. Then the variable mark is assigned a value of 100 through the pointer variable pmark and a dereferencing operator. After the assignment of value 100, the same dereferencing mechanism is applied on pointer pmark to get the data of mark for output. Hence, the statement

*cout<<*pmark;*

has the same effect as in the following statement:

cout<<mark;

This task of accessing the data through pointers is also known as indirect addressing.

CHAPTER SEVEN

User Defined Functions in C++

A function is a sub program, which performs a specific task using the values given as input and then returns the result to the calling program. It contains a set of program statements that can be processed independently. When a function is invoked or called from other part of the program, it behaves as though its code is inserted at the point of the function call.

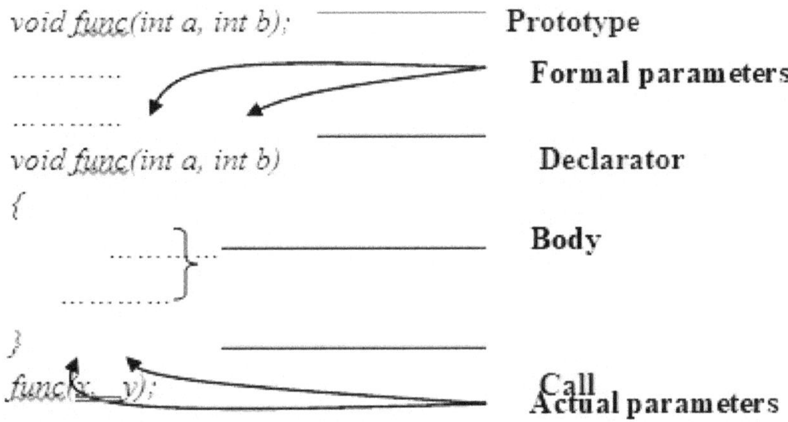

Fig. 7.1: Components of a Function

The program, which calls a function, is called as 'Caller', and the function being called is known as 'Callee'. The communication between the caller and the callee takes place through a set of variables called parameters. Functions are independent when the variables used within its body are local to it.

Every function has the following elements associated with it:

1. Function declaration or prototype
2. Function parameters (formal parameters)
3. Combination of function declaration and its definition
4. Return statement and
5. Function call

Function Prototype:

This component is a declaration statement, which provides the following information to the compiler:

- The name of the function
- The type of the value returned (optional; default is an integer)
- The number and types of the arguments that must be supplied in a call to the function

When a function call is encountered, the compiler checks the function call with its prototype in order to ensure that the arguments used in function call are of proper data type. The function prototype is having the following syntax:

"*ret_val function_name (argument 1, argument 2, ……, argument n);*"

In this syntax, the ret_val specifies the data type of the value to be returned. When a function does not return any value, it must be specified with a keyword void. A void function can include a dummy return statement to return the control back to its caller without returning any value. The default return type is integer.

An example for function declaration is as follows:

"*int max(int x, int y);*"

In this example, int is the data type of the return value, max is the name of the function, and x and y are arguments of type int. It is also noted that the function declaration is end with a semicolon.

C++ makes prototyping mandatory if functions are defined after the function main(), i.e., after the function call. It assumes void in case of no arguments in the argument list.

Function Definition:

The function itself is referred to as function definition. The first line of the function definition is known as function declarator or function header and is followed by the function body, which is enclosed in braces.

C++ allows the definition to be placed anywhere in the program. If the function is defined before its invocation, then its prototype declaration is optional. The following figure shows a valid function definition:

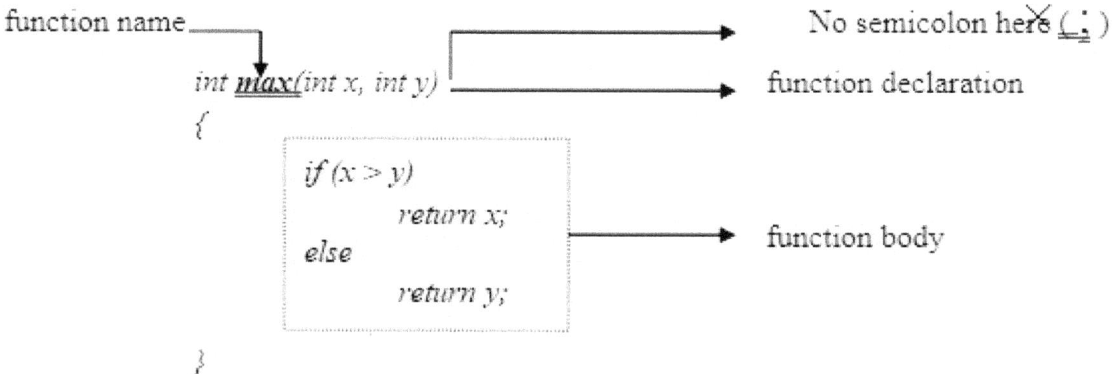

Fig. 7.2: Function Definition of Function max()

Function body should contain a return statement to return the control back to its caller. The return statement can also be used to return the result of the function to its caller. The following is the syntax for a function that doesn't return any value:

"*void fnName(param-list)*
{

statement(s)
return; // return is optional
}"

The following figure shows the function max( ) returning a value to the caller:

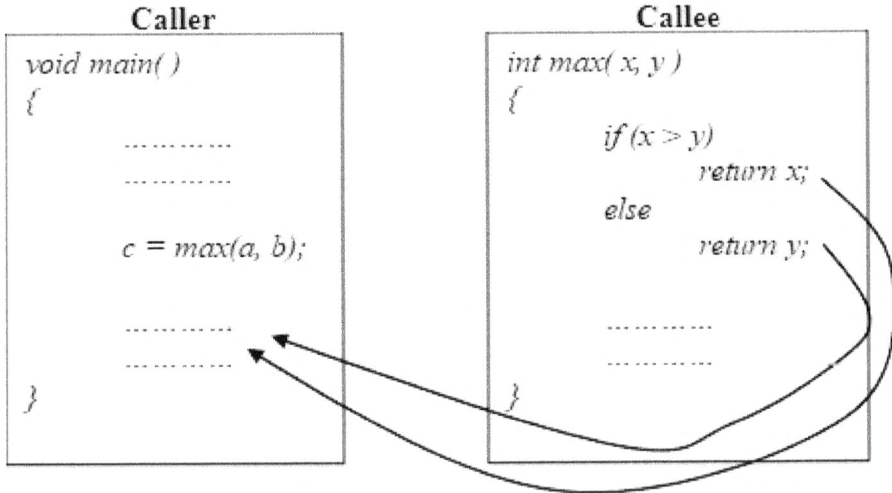

Fig. 7.3: Function max() with return Statement

When the return type is void, the function need not return any value, i.e., there is no need for a return statement within the function body.

Types of C++ functions

C++ functions are of two types: Non-member function and Member function. They are classified based on the area of their declaration in a program. The functions that are declared in the public declaration area (i.e., outside main()) are called non-member functions and the functions that are declared inside a class (i.e., functions belong to a class) are called member functions.

Non-member functions:

A non-member function is a C++ function, which is declared in the public declaration area of the program. The definition of a non-member function is written usually after the function main(). If it is placed before the function main() or before the point of its invocation, the declaration part can be omitted.

Normally, a function returns a value to its caller. When the return type is not specified in the function header, it is assumed to be integer. Every function that returns a value should have one or more return statements. The return statement can be used for transferring the control back to the caller with a result.

When a function returns no value to its caller, its return type must be specified as void in the function header. A function that doesn't return any value can have an empty return statement or not.

Member Function:

Member function is a function that belongs to a class. It is declared inside the class, but can be defined either inside or outside the class. A member function, which is declared inside and defined outside the class, separates the declaration part of the function from its implementation.

In general, C++ member functions are declared and stored in a file called Header file (.H), and are coded and implemented in another file called program file (.CPP).

Main() in C++:

The function main() is the starting point of execution in every C++ program. It takes its input through arguments from the command line of the OS and returns its result back to the OS. Thus, it is expected in every main function to have a return statement with an integer value to indicate the success or failure of its statements.

Many OS tests the return value (called exit value) to determine if there is any problem in executing the program. The normal convention is that an exit value of zero means the program ran successfully, while a non-zero value means there was a problem.

The definition of main() would look like this:

```
"main() {
  // main program statements
  }"
```

The function main() will return the control back to the caller (here, it is OS) when it encounters a closing brace or a return statement. And hence, the above version of function main() can be furnished as follows:

```
"int main() {
  ..................
  ..................
  return 0;
  }"
```

Following is an example for making a function call in C++. The following program uses a function called max() to find the maximum of two integers.

```
#include<iostram.h>
int max(int x, int y);
int main() {
int a, b, c;
cout<<"Enter two integers (a & b) :";
cin>>a>>b;
cout<<"The Maximum of given integers is:"<<c<<endl;
return 0;
}
int max(int x, int y) {
if(x>y)
return x;
else
return y;
}
```

SECTION II - Object Oriented Programming in C++

Section II explains the topics related to OOP in C++ that include: Classes and Objects, Function Overload and Operator Overloading, Inheritance, Virtual Functions, Input Output Handling, File Handling and Exception Handling.

Topics covered in Section II are as follows:

- Introduction to Class and Object in C++
- Creating and Using Objects in C++
- Implementing Operator Overloading in C++
- Inheritance and its implementation
- Virtual and Pure Virtual Functions in C++

CHAPTER EIGHT

Introducing Class and Object in C++

Object oriented programming involves the following three steps:

1. Declaration of classes for defining objects and their behavior
2. Creation of class objects using their class definition and
3. Establishment of communication among objects through message passing.

An object-oriented program consists of collection of objects that interact with each other. An object is a stand-alone entity, the collection of which can accomplish a particular task. Objects are nothing but instances or variables of a user-defined data type called class.

A class is a user defined data type, which defines the object by specifying the type and scope of all its members. The members of a class are of two types: variables and functions. The variables define the data of an object and are called as data members, where as the functions determine the operations to be performed on the data of an object and are called as member functions.

The syntax of class specification is as follows:

```
"class ClassName
  {
  // body of the class
  };"
```

where, class is a keyword and ClassName is an identifier given for the new data type of class. The keyword class indicates that the name, which follows (ClassName) is an abstract data type. The body of the class is enclosed within a pair of curly braces and is followed by a semicolon, which specifies the end of the class specification.

Access Specifiers:

Access specifiers are keywords used for specifying the scope or area within which a member of a class can be directly or freely accessed. There are three access specifiers in C++: private, protected and public. They control the visibility status of the members of a class.

The members of a class are defined under any one of the scope specifiers. The private and protected members are accessible only to their own class' members. On the other hand, public members are accessible from both inside and outside the class.

The class members declared in the private scope are accessible to only members of its own class in order to protect the data from unauthorized access. But, the members declared under public or protected scope are accessible from objects of the class, in addition to their own class members.

Generally, data members are declared as private variables and member functions as public functions of a class. Hence, the default scope (the scope when not specified) of a class member is private, i.e., the members (data & functions) are considered as private members, unless otherwise specified.

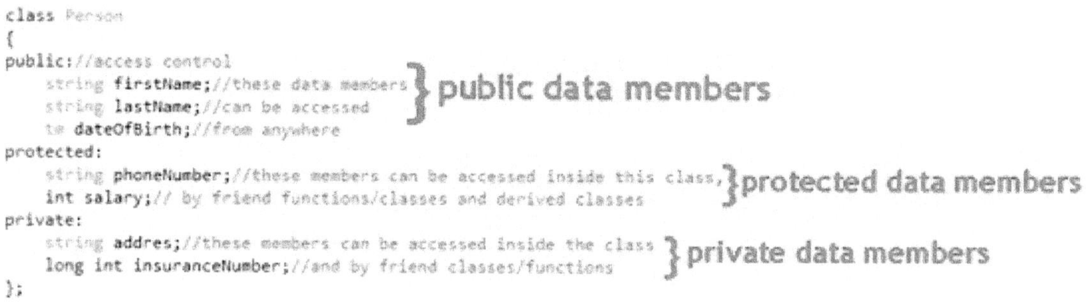

```
class Person
{
public://access control
    string firstName;//these data members      } public data members
    string lastName;//can be accessed
    tm dateOfBirth;//from anywhere
protected:
    string phoneNumber;//these members can be accessed inside this class,   } protected data members
    int salary;// by friend functions/classes and derived classes
private:
    string addres;//these members can be accessed inside the class   } private data members
    long int insuranceNumber;//and by friend classes/functions
};
```

Fig. 8.1: Decaring Members of a Class with various Access Scpeifiers

This is the major difference between the data type structure and class: the members of a structure are public in nature, whereas, in class, they are private by default. The following is a specification of Student object:

```
class Student{
int roll_no;
char name[20];
public:
void SetData(int proll_no, char *pname)
{
roll_no = proll_no;
name = pname;
}
void OutData()
{
cout<< "Roll No = " << roll_no << endl;
cout<< "Name = " << name << endl;
}
};
```

In this example, the class Student is defined with four members: roll_no, name, SetData() and OutData() (i.e., two data members and two member functions). The data members roll_no and name are declared as private variables and hence they can't be directly accessed from outside the class. They can be only accessed by the member functions of the class.

The member functions SetData and OutData are defined under public scope so that they can be accessed from outside the class. They contain the statements for assigning and retrieving data from the private data members of the class.

Member Function Declaration:

Member functions are functions declared inside a class; and defined either inside or outside the class. When defined inside the class, they are known as inline functions. Member functions defined outside the class use the class name followed by :: (scope resolution operator) as prefix to the function name in its header.

An inline function is expanded in line when it is invoked, i.e., the compiler replaces the function call with the corresponding function code. The functions, which are defined outside the class are called non-inline member functions and are invoked as ordinary functions during the function call. Following is an example for defining the member functions both inside and outside the class:

```
#include <iostream.h>
```

```
class Item{
int number;
float cost;
public:
void GetData(int a, float b);
void PutData(void) {
cout << "Item Number : " << number << "\n";
cout << "Item Cost : " << cost << "\n";
}
};
void Item :: GetData(int a, float b) {
number = a;
cost = b;
}
int main() {
item x;
cout << "Enter No. and Cost for Item x" << "\n";
x.GetData(100, 299.95);
x.PutData();
item y;
cout << "Enter No. and Cost for Item y" << "\n";
y.GetData(200, 175.50);
y.PutData();
}
```

In this example, two member functions are declared namely GetData and PutData. The function GetData() is an in-line function, whereas the function PutData() is a non-inline function.

Member functions are called from outside the class using the object variable and a dot (.) operator as prefix to the function name. The member functions have some special characteristics that are often used in the program development. They are:

1. Several different classes can have member functions with a same name.
2. Member functions can access the private data of a class, whereas, non-member functions can't do so.
3. A member function can call another member function directly, without using the dot operator.

Generally, member functions are declared as public members of a class. But, sometimes they are declared in the private section of the class. Such functions are called as private member functions. They can only be accessed within the class as private data members.

Types of Member Functions

The member functions, which are declared inside the class, are further classified into five types:

1. Inline member functions
2. Constructors
3. Destructors
4. Static member functions and
5. Friend functions

Inline functions:

Inline functions are member functions, which are interpreted and executed in the same line of its function call. They are declared inside the class, but defined inside or outside the class.

When a member function is both declared and defined inside the class, it becomes an inline function. To define an inline function outside the class, prefix the function header with the keyword inline.

Normally, during a function call, the flow of execution (control flow) of the program is transferred from the current line of the program to the first line of the function for its execution. After the completion of function execution, the control will be brought back to the same line, where the function call occurred to resume the normal flow of execution.

Inline functions are executed in a different way from the normal function execution. They are executed in the same line of its function call, because during compile time, the compiler interprets and replaces the function call with the actual body of the function itself. So, there is no need for control transfer to the function for its execution incase of inline function.

Following is an example program for using inline functions in C++:

```
#include <iostram.h>
class Date{
int dd;
int mm;
int yy;
public:
void SetDate(int day, int month, int year){
dd = day;
mm = month;
yy = year;
}
void ShowDate( );
};
inline void Date::ShowDate( )
{
cout<< dd << " / " << mm << " / " << yy << endl;
}
void main(){
Date DOI;
DOI.SetDate(15, 8, 1947);
cout << "Our Independance day is : ";
DOI.ShowDate();
}
```

In this example, both member functions SetDate and ShowDate are declared as inline functions. Because, the function SetDate is defined inside the class, and the function ShowDate is defined outside the class with the keyword inline as prefix.

From main(), these two functions are called to set the date of independence and to display it. At the time of compilation, the compiler will replace these two function calls with the body of their corresponding function as follows:

```
void main()
{
Date DOI;
```

```
dd = 15;
mm = 08;
yy = 1947;
cout << "Our Independence day is : ";
cout<< dd << " / " << mm << " / " << yy << endl;
}
```

When to use Inline functions?

In general, inline functions should not be used. But, occasionally C++ programmers use them. The following are the scenario in which inline functions are used effectively:

Inline functions can be used when a fully developed and tested program works too slowly and shows bottlenecks in certain functions.

An inline function is beneficial to a program when it consists of one very simple statement like return.

It can be used in a program, if the time spent during a function call is more, compared to the time taken for executing the function. The statements used in the function body must be simple and should take less time for processing.

Constructors:

Constructor is a special member function having the same name of its class and is executed automatically at the time of object creation (instantiating an object). It is used mainly to initialize the data members of an object and to allocate necessary resources for it.

Constructor is executed every time a new object is instantiated. It is of course possible to define a class, which has no constructor; in such a case, the run-time system calls a dummy constructor (i.e., a constructor that performs no action) during object creation. The rules to be followed while defining a constructor is as follows:

Constructors must be declared inside a class and also under the public scope. But, they can be defined either within, or outside the body of the class like other members.

Constructors can take zero or more parameters for initialization, but return no value. Therefore, there is no specification for the return type of constructor in its header (not even void). For instance, for the class Bag, the constructor is this:

“*Bag :: Bag() { }*”

Constructors can be overloaded with the same name but different parameters. The constructor, which takes no argument is called default constructor. The default constructor is called when no parameters are passed to the object while its creation; otherwise a parameterized constructor that matches its parameters with the number and type of arguments passed to the object will be called to initialize the object.

Destructors:

Destructor is also a member function like constructor and takes the same name of the class, but proceeded by the character ~ (tilde). It will be invoked automatically when the object is deleted or goes out of scope. It generally contains the code to reclaim all the resources allocated to the object.

Following are the rules to be considered while defining a destructor for a class:

- The destructor function has the same name of its class but prefixed by a tilde (~). The tilde distinguishes it from the constructor of the same class.

- Unlike the constructor, the destructor does not take any arguments. This is because there is only one way to destroy an object.
- The destructor has neither arguments, nor a return value.
- The destructor has no return type like constructor, since it is invoked automatically whenever an object goes out of scope.
- There can be only one destructor in each class. This is essentially a violation of the rule that a function can take arguments, thereby making function overloading impossible.

String Class using Constructor and Destructor:

The following is a C++ program that defines a class named String with two constructors, one destructor and a member function Display():

```
#include<iostream.h>
#include<string.h>
static const SSIZE = 50;
class String
{
char *str;
public:
String()
{
str = new char[SSIZE];
str = "Default Constructor";
}
String(char* ps)
{
str = new char[strlen(ps)];
strcpy(str, ps);
}
void Display()
{
cout<<str<<endl;
}
~String(){
delete str;
}
};
void main(){
clrscr();
String name1;
String name2 = "Parameterized Constructor";
String name3 = name2;
name1.Display();
name2.Display();
name3.Display();
}
```

CHAPTER NINE

Creating and Using Objects in C++

Class objects are nothing but objects (or instances) created using the specification provided in a class data type. A class is a specification, which defines the structure of an object or object(s).

A class must be instantiated first, before making use of the services provided in it. For instantiating a class, we need to declare a variable of type class. This process of creating an object after its definition (using class) is called class instantiation.

Creating objects of a class can be done in three different ways:

1. Declaring an object variable along with its definition (class declaration).
2. Defining the class and declaring its variable in two different statements (i.e., two lines of code).
3. Using an object pointer and the new keyword.

At the time of object instantiation, necessary resources like memory and I/O devices are allocated to it. An example for the first method is as follows:

```
class Student{
int roll_no;
char name[20];
public:
void SetData(int proll_no, char *pname);
void OutData();
} S1, S2, S3, S4;
```

The following is an example code for class instantiation using the second method:

```
class Student{
int roll_no;
char name[20];
public:
void SetData(int proll_no, char *pname);
void OutData();
};
class Student S1, S2, S3, S4;
(or)
Student S1, S2, S3, S4;
```

Using the first method, declaration of both class (Student) and its objects (S1, S2, S3, S4) are done in a single line of statement. But, with the second method, the class declaration and its object creation are separated and put in two lines.

The third way of creating an object is by declaring an object pointer and assigning it with the address of a newly created object using the new keyword. The example is as follows:

```
class Student{
int roll_no;
```

```
char name[20];
public:
void SetData(int proll_no, char *pname);
void OutData();
};
class Student *S = new Student;
```

Accessing Class Members:

Once an object is created using an object variable or an object pointer, its public members can be accessed through an operator. There are two operators provided in C++ for accessing the members of an object: dot (.) operator and indirection (-->) operator. The dot operator (.) is used to access the members of an object variable, whereas the indirection operator (-->) is used for accessing the members of an object through its pointer.

Syntax for accessing the data members of a class is as follows:

"*ObjectName.DataMember*
(or)
ObjectName--> DataMember"

If the member to be accessed is a function, then a pair of parenthesis enclosing zero or more parameters is to be added following the function name as given below:

"*ObjectName.MemberFunction(Actual Parameters)*"

Examples for calling the member function of an object are as follows:

```
Student S1;
S1.SetData(10, "Raj");
S1.OutData();
(or)
Student *pS = new Student;
pS -->SetData(10, "Raj");
pS-->OutData();
```

Message Passing between Objects:

A message for an object is interpreted as a request for executing an operation. A subroutine or a function is invoked soon after receiving a message and the desired results are generated within the object. This process of passing messages between two objects in a program is done based on a model called Client/Server model.

In Client/Server model, a client is an object or a function like main, which sends the message as a request to an object called server that provides services to the client in the form of functions.

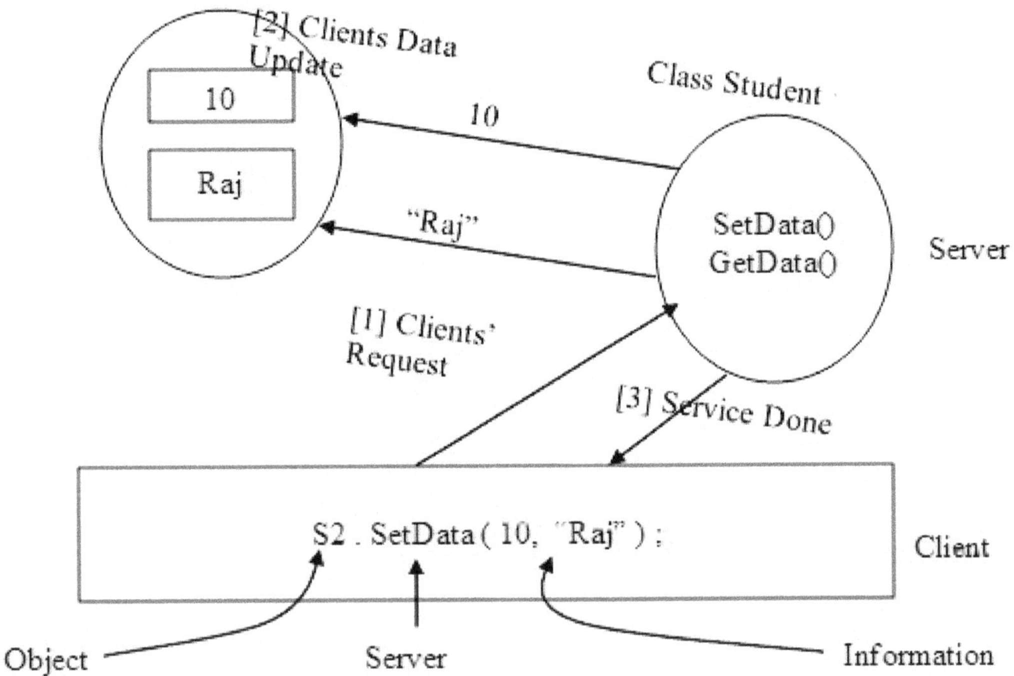

Fig. 9.1: Accessing the Members of an Object using . (dot) Operator

In the above figure, the server is the class named Student. It contains the functions *SetData()* and *GetData()* for storing and retrieving the details RollNo and Name of one or more students. The client is the *main()* function, which calls the service *SetData* of object S2.

Calling a service from the client is the first process takes places as shown in the above figure. The server responds to the client's request by performing the function GetData on the object S2. The values 10 and "Raj" are passed as parameters while requesting the server. The server updates the object S2 with the values given as parameters. Then the server gives an acknowledgement (the result) back to the client i.e., a return value, which specifies the success or failure of the function call.

Following is a C++ program that defines a 'point' object with two data members: x and y and two member function getxy() and showxy():

```
# include <iostream.h>
class point
{
private:
float x, y;
public:
void getxy()
{
cout << "Enter the coordinates x and y:";
cin >> x >> y;
}
void showxy()
{
cout << "X coordinate :" << x << endl;
cout << "Y coordinate :" << x << endl;
```

```
}
};
void main()
{
point p1, p2;
cout << "Enter the coordinates for Point 1;" << endl;
p1.getxy();
cout << "Enter the coordinates for Point 2;" << endl;
p2.getxy();
cout << "Point 1 contains"<< endl;
p1.showxy();
cout << "Point 2 contains"<< endl;
p2.showxy();
}
```

In this program, we have a class named point, which defines two properties x and y of type float and two member function getxy() and showxy(). The data members are of type float and are hidden. The public members getxy() and showxy() act as interfaces to the local members x and y in order to store and retrieve values from them.

In function main(), we have two objects p1 and p2 to store the coordinates of a line. With the help of these objects, we get the coordinates for a line and then display them one by one. To display some prompt string like "Enter the coordinates x and y for point 1", we use cout statements in the program.

Friend Class:

A friend class is a class that is declared as a friend to another class. The friend class can have a member function with a reference to the other class through which it can access the private members of its friend. The following is an example program for illustrating the use of friend member function and a friend class:

```
#include <iostram.h>
class A{
private:
int data;
public:
void SetData(int d){
data = d;
}
int GetData(){
return(data);
}
friend void Incr(A a);
friend class B;
};
void Incr(A &a)
{
a.data++;
}
class B{
int data;
public:
void Add(A &a){
```

```
data += a.data;
}
void SetData(int d){
data = d;
}
int GetData(){
return(data);
}
};
void main(){
A objA;
objA.SetData(5);
Incr(objA);
B objB;
objB.SetData(10);
objB.Add(objA);
cout<<objB.GetData();
}
```

The output of this program is 16. This program uses two classes A and B. Class A has a friend function named Incr and a friend class B. Class B is declared as a friend to class A so that it can freely access the private members of class A, but through a reference. In class B, we have a member function which takes a reference to class A as its parameter through which it will access the private member (data) of class A.

The friend function *Incr()* of class A is declared as a public member, and is defined outside the class as a non-member function with out using scope specifier. When used from function *main()*, it is called as though it is a non-member function (without dot operator).

In function *main()*, objA is created first with a value of 5. Then, the friend function Incr is called with a reference to *objA* to increment the value to 6. Next, *objB* is created with an initial value 10. This is followed by a function call Add() using objB along with a reference to *objA*, which will store resultant value 16 in *objB*.

More Elements of OOP in C++

Elements are nothing but programming constructs that actually implement the concepts introduced in Object Orientation. Some of the major concepts introduced by OOP are: data abstraction, encapsulation, polymorphism and inheritance. These concepts are implemented in OOP languages like C++ and Java using various programming constructs such as class, object, function overloading, function overriding and operator overloading.

Classes and objects are the two major elements of OOP, which implement the concepts of abstraction, encapsulation and message passing. The other concepts such as polymorphism, inheritance and persistence are implemented using the following elements of the OOP:

- Function overloading and Operator overloading
- Derived and Parent class (Inheritance)
- Virtual and Overridden member functions
- Pure Virtual functions and Abstract Base class
- Dynamic memory allocation

Function Overloading:

Function overloading is an element of OOP, which implements the concept called Polymorphism. The word polymorphism is derived from the Greek meaning many forms. A word is said to be overloaded when it has two or more distinct meaning. The intended meaning of any particular word is determined by its context.

In function overloading, two or more functions can be given the same name provided each has a unique signature. Overloaded functions differ in the number of arguments they take or in the data type of their arguments used for parameter passing. The selection of one of the overloaded member functions during function call is resolved at compile time based on the number and data types of actual parameters used in the function call.

The following is an example for function overloading in C++:

```
#include <iostream.h>
class Poly {
void Show(int val)
{
cout << "Integer : " << val << endl;
}
void Show(double val)
{
cout << "Double : " << val << endl;
}
void Show(char *val)
{
cout << "String : " << val << endl;
}
};
int main(){
Poly p;
p.Show(420);
p.Show(3.1415);
p.Show("Hello, World!");
return(0);
}
```

In this program, three functions are defined in the class Poly with the same name *Show()*, but with different arguments. The first function has the argument of type int, the second one has the argument type double and the third function's argument is of type *char**. Such functions are called as overloaded functions.

When an overloaded function is called from a function like main, the selection of the appropriate overloaded function takes place based on the argument passed during the function call. Moreover, the compiler does this selection process during compile time. Thus, this type of polymorphism is called as Compile-time Polymorphism.

In the above example, the overloaded function *Show()* is called thrice from the function main(), but with different arguments. During first call, the function is called with data - 420, which is of type integer. This will invoke the function with integer argument. Similarly, other overloaded functions are invoked during the second and third function call.

CHAPTER TEN

Operator Overloading

An operator is a symbol used for performing certain operation on the operands given for it. It can be considered as a function that performs its operation on the operands passed as parameters to it. Operators help us to reduce the need for unusual functions and make the code easier to understand.

Using operator overloading, operators such as +, -, * and /, which deal with basic data types, can be extended to work on user-defined data type like String and Date. Overloaded operators work with ordinary variables as well as object variables and the selection of operation to be performed is based on the type of operators used for the operator.

Function overloading allows a programmer to call many functions with the same name but different parameters, whereas operator overloading allows a single operator to be associated with different operations depending on the type of data given as operands. It also extends the semantics of an operator without changing their syntax.

Example for operator overloading is string concatenation using an operator that adds or combines two strings into one. To concatenate two strings, we can use the arithmetic operator +, by overloading it to do such operation as follows:

> "*char firstName[20], lastName[20], Name[40];*
> *Name = firstName + lastName;*"

Operator overloading, thus allows a programmer to provide additional meaning to the operators such as +, *, >=, +=, << and >>, when they are applied to user defined data types. When used for extending the capacity of the standard operator, it extends the semantics of an operator without changing its syntax.

The grammatical rules that govern its use such as the number of operands, precedence, and associativity of the operator remain the same for overloaded operators. This concept of operator overloading can also be applied to data conversion.

Overloadable Operators:

C++ allows almost all operators (both unary and binary) to be overloaded. When overloading an operator, at least one operand of the overloaded operator must be an instance of a class (object). Operator overloading is implemented in a class using a function called Operator Function.

Operator function is a member function of a class having the keyword operator in its header, and is preceded by a return type. The operator to be overloaded is written immediately after the keyword operator. The syntax of the operator function is as follows:

```
"ReturnType operator OperatorSymbol([arg1, [arg2]])
 {
 //body of operator function
 }"
```

where,

ReturnType - may be primitive or void or user-defined data type

operator - is a keyword that informs the compiler that the following function is a function written for overloading an operator.

OperatorSymbol - is any one of the overloadable unary or binary operator in C++

arg1, arg2, ... - are optional arguments of either primitive or user defined data type.

The following is a list of operators that can be overloaded in C++:

<table>
<tr><th>Operator Category</th><th>Operators</th></tr>
<tr><td>Arithmetic</td><td>+, -, *, /, %</td></tr>
<tr><td>Bit Wise</td><td>&, |, ~, ^</td></tr>
<tr><td>Logical</td><td>&&, ||, !</td></tr>
<tr><td>Relational</td><td><, >, ==, !=, <=, >=</td></tr>
<tr><td>Assignment (or) Initialization</td><td>=</td></tr>
<tr><td>Arithmetic Assignment</td><td>+=, -=, *=, /=, %=, &=, !=, ^=</td></tr>
<tr><td>Shift</td><td><<, >>, <<=, >>=</td></tr>
<tr><td>Unary</td><td>++, --</td></tr>
<tr><td>Function Call</td><td>()</td></tr>
<tr><td>Dereferencing</td><td>→·</td></tr>
<tr><td>Unary Sign Prefix</td><td>+, -</td></tr>
<tr><td>Allocate and Free</td><td>new, delete</td></tr>
</table>

Fig. 10.1: List of Overloadable Operators in C++

Unary and Binary Operator Overloading:

An operator function written without any argument is known as Unary Operator Overloading, whereas an operator function with a single explicit argument is known as Binary Operator Overloading. However, with friend functions, unary operators take one explicit argument and binary operators take two explicit arguments.

The syntax for invoking the overloaded unary operator function is as follows:

"*Object Operator*
Operator Object "

The first syntax invokes the function for performing a prefix operation and the second syntax calls the function for a postfix operation. The syntax for invoking the overloaded binary operator function is as follows:

"*Object1 Operator Object2* "

For instance, the expression obj1 + obj2 invokes the overloaded member function (operator function) + of the first object (Object1) by passing the Object2 as its parameter. It is interpreted as follows:

"*Object1.operator +(Object 2);* "

The following is an example for overloading arithmetic operators on a class data type named String:

```
#include <iostream.h>
#include <string.h>
const int BUFF_SIZE = 50;
class String
{
private:
char str[BUFF_SIZE];
public:
String(){
strcpy(str, " ");
}
String(char *pStr){
strcpy(str, pStr);
}
void Echo(){
cout << str;
}
void Read(){
cin >> str;
}
String operator +(String S)
{
String temp = str;
strcat(str, s.str);
return temp;
}
boolean operator >(String s)
{
if (strcmp(str, s.str) < 0)
return TRUE;
else
return FALSE;
}
boolean operator <(String s)
{
if (strcmp(str, s.str) > 0)
return TRUE;
else
return FALSE;
}
```

```
boolean operator ==(String s)
{
if (strcmp(str, s.str) == 0)
return TRUE;
else
return FALSE;
}
};
void main()
{
String str1, str2;
cout << "Enter two Strings :";
str1.Read();
str2.Read();
if (str1 == str2)
cout << "The Strings are equal";
else
{
if(str1 < str2)
cout << "The string " + str1 + "stands first in the order";
else
cout << "The string " + str2 + "stands first in the order";
}
cout << "The concatenated String is : " << str1 + str2;
}
```

In the above example, the class String has four operator functions: +, <, > and == for performing the operations - concatenation and comparison on strings. It also has other members functions - Echo(), Read() and two constructors (default and parameter constructor).

From function main, two objects str1 and str2 are instantiated to store, compare and concatenate two strings. Using the operator == they are compared to see if are equal; if not, the ordeal position of the strings is compared using the operator <. Finally, the two strings are concatenated and displayed using the operator +.

Implementing Unary and Binary Operators on Strings:

The following is a C++ program that overloads the unary operator– (reversing a string) and binary operator + (string concatenation) on String data type without using String functions - strcmp() and strcat():

```
#include <iostream.h>
class String
{
public:
char *str;
String(){
Str = new char[50];
str = "\0";
}
String(char* ps){
Str = new char[strlen(ps)];
str = ps;
```

```
}
char* operator+(String s)
{
Int ls1, ls2;
char* ts;
ls1 = strlen(str);
ls2 = strlen(s.str);
ts = new char[ls1 + ls2 + 1];
for(int i=0; I < ls1; i++)
ts[i] = str[i];
for(int j=0; j < ls2; j++)
ts[i] = s.str[j];
return ts;
}
char* operator –()
{
Int len;
char* ts;
len = strlen(str);
ts = new char[len+1];
for(int i=0; i<= len; i++)
ts[i] = str[len – i – 1];
ts[i] = str[i];
return ts;
}
char* Echo(){
return str;
}
};
void main()
{
String name1("OOP");
cout<<"The Reverse String is : " << –name1;
String name2(" in C++");
cout<<"The Concatenated String is : " << name1+name2;
}
```

The output of this program will be:

POO

OOP in C++

Non-Overloadable C++ Operators:

The following is a list of non-overload able operators in C++:

Operator Category	Operators
Member Access	. (dot operator)
Scope Resolution	:: (global access)
Conditional	?: (conditional statement)
Pointer to Member	*
Size of Data Type	sizeof(...)

Fig. 10.2: Non-Overloadable Operators in C++

CHAPTER ELEVEN

Inheritance and its Implementation in C++

Reusability is one of the important features of OOP, which allows the user to reuse classes that already exists rather than creating the same all over again. This feature results in reduced cost and time and increased reliability of the program being developed.

Once a class has been written and tested, it can be adapted by other programmers to suit their requirements. Reusability is achieved by creating new classes using the properties and methods of existing classes. This mechanism of deriving a new class from an old one is called inheritance or derivation.

Inheritance is a technique of organizing classes in a hierarchical form. It allows new classes to be built from older and less specialized classes instead of being rewritten from scratch. In this process, the old class is referred to as the base class and the new class as the derived class.

The following figure shows the relationship between a base class and its derived class through inheritance:

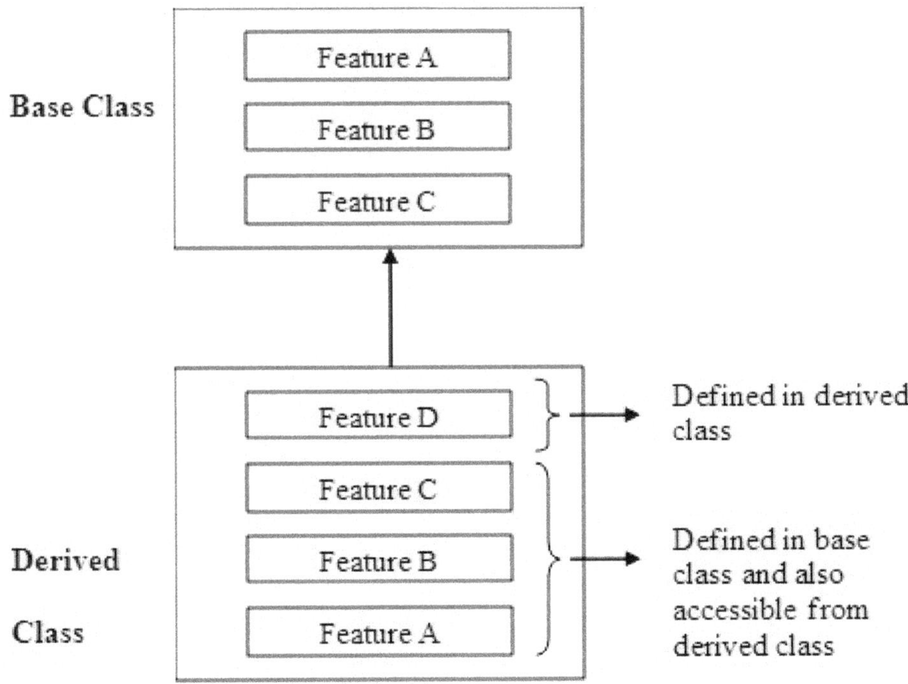

Fig. 11.1: Deriving a New Class From an Existing Class in C++

The arrow in the diagram symbolizes derived from. Its direction from the derived class towards the base class represents that the derived class accesses features of the base class not vice versa.

The derived class inherits all the capabilities of the base class with some refinements and extensions of its own. The base class remains unchanged. A base class is often called the Ancestor, Parent or Super Class and a derived class is called the Descendent, Child or Sub Class. A derived may also be used as a base class from which additional classes are derived.

Types of Inheritance:

There are five types of inheritance supported in C++:

1. Single inheritance
2. Multiple inheritance
3. Hierarchical inheritance
4. Multilevel inheritance
5. Hybrid inheritance

A class which is derived from single base class is called single inheritance, and a class with several base classes is called multiple inheritance. On the other hand, deriving a new class from another derived class is known as multi-level inheritance.

In hierarchical inheritance, one base class is used for deriving multiple derived classes. In hybrid inheritance, we have a mix of all other types of inheritance.

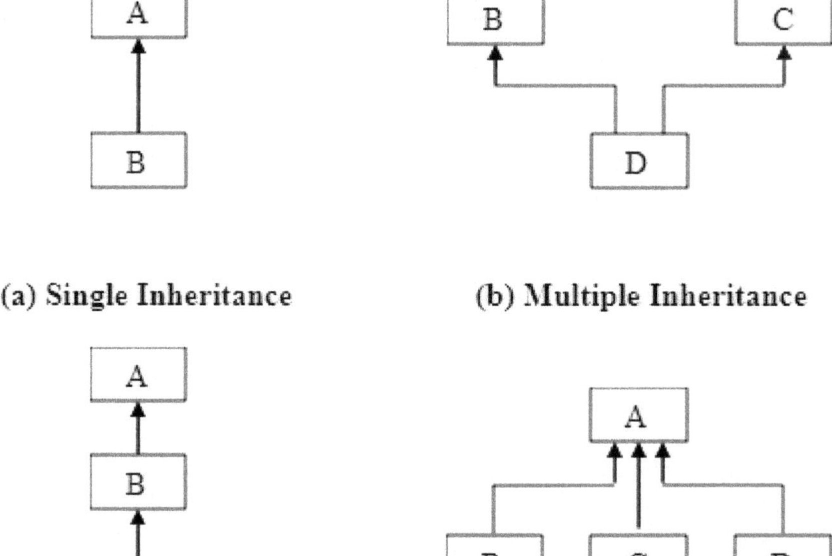

(a) Single Inheritance **(b) Multiple Inheritance**

(c) Multi-level Inheritance **(d) Hierarchical Inheritance**

Fig. 11.2: Inheritance Types - Single, Multiple, Multi-level and Hierarchical

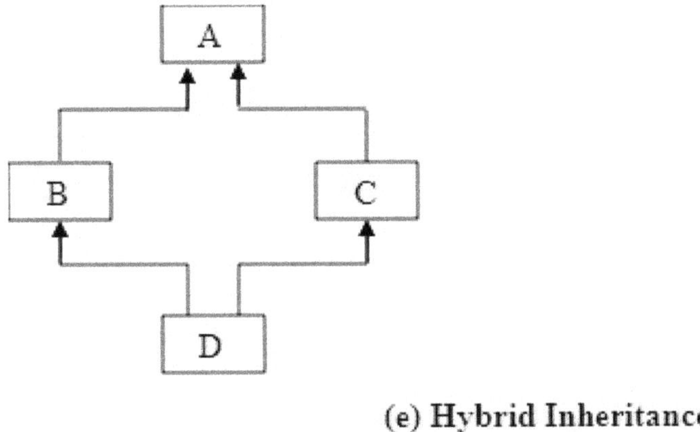

(e) Hybrid Inheritance

Fig. 11.3: Hybrid type of Inheritance in C++

Access specifier - Protected:

Like private members, protected members are having private scope in accessing its members, i.e., they can be accessed only within the class. Unlike private members, they can be derived and accessed from a derived class (outside the parent class). Thus, the protected scope of a parent class gives its members protection from public access, but at the same time freedom of inheritance to its derived class.

The following are the differences among three scope specifiers used in class declaration:

Scope Specifiers	Meaning
Private	Visible only to the member functions of a class but not in its derived class.
Protected	Makes its members visible to member functions of the same class and also its derived class.
Public	This scope exposes its members to member functions within the class, its derived class and also to the external world (outside the class).

Fig. 11.4: Role of Scope Speicifers in Inheritance

Declaring a Derived Class:

A derived class extends its features by inheriting the properties of another class, called base class and adding features of its own. The syntax of declaring a derived class is as follows:

"*class DerivedClass : [Visibility Mode] BaseClass {*

//members of derived class
}; "

In this syntax, the derivation of DerivedClass from the BaseClass is indicated by the colon (:). The visibility mode, which is optional, indicates the type of inheritance (public or private). It specifies the scope of the inherited members in the derived class. The default scope is private, i.e., when not specified, members (both public and protected) of the base class are inherited into the private scope of the derived class. If it is specified, it must be public or private.

Inheritance of a base class with visibility mode public causes the public members of the base class to become the public members of the derived class and the protected members of the base class become protected members of the derived class. Hence, the objects of the derived class can access only the public members of the base class that are inherited publicly.

The private members of the base class remain private to the base class, in both private and public inheritance. Derived class can access them only through the inherited member functions of the base class. The following table lists out the visibility modes and their usage in deriving a new class from an existing one:

Base Class Visibility	**Derived Class Visibility**	
	Public Derivation	**Private Derivation**
Private	Not Inherited	Not Inherited
Protected	Protected	Private
Public	Public	Private

Fig. 11.5: Area of Visibility Determined by Scope Specifiers during Inheritance

From the above table, it is concluded that if a class is expected to be used as a base class in the future, its derivable members must be declared under protected scope and the class must be inherited publicly by its descendants.

An example for deriving a new class from an existing one is as follows:

```
class Account
{
float amount;
public:
void Deposit(amount);
void Withdraw(amount);
}
class Savings : public Account
{
char type;
}
```

In this example, there are two classes: Account, and Savings. Account is a parent class, and Savings is a derived class. The parent class defines one private data member (amount) and two member functions (Deposit and Withdraw). The derived class inherits all the public members of the base class; in addition it includes one private data named type.

The derived class Savings in the above example has the visibility mode public for its derived members. Hence, the derived class will have one private member (type) and two public members (Deposit and Withdraw), which are derived from the base class.

Constructors in Derived Class

Derived class need not have a constructor as long as the base class has a default constructor. Default constructors are automatically invoked both in the base class and in the derived class in this order –base class first and then the derived class. However, if the base class has constructors with arguments (one or more), then it is mandatory for the derived class to have a constructor so as to pass the arguments to the base class constructor. Suppose the base class has only argument constructors, then they must be invoked explicitly; otherwise the compiler generates an error.

The following example illustrates the explicit invocation of the argument constructor of the base class:

```
#include <iostream.h>
class B{
protected:
int b;
public:
B(){
b = 0;
cout << "Default constructor of the Base Class is invoked"
}
B(int a){
b = a;
cout << "One-argument constructor of the Base Class is invoked";
}
};
class D : public B{
public:
D(int a) : B(a)
{
cout << "One-argument constrctor of the Derived Class is invoked";
}
};
void main()
{
D objd;
D objD(3);
}
```

In this example, there are two constructors for the base class B. One is a default constructor, and the other one is a parameterized constructor with an integer argument a. In the derived class, there is only one constructor, which is a parameterized constructor with an integer argument a. The use of this constructor is to invoke the base class parameterized constructor with an argument for initialization.

The function main() has an object named objD, which is created using the derived class D along with an integer constant (3). This will invoke the base class parameterized constructor explicitly through the derived class parameterized constructor along with the value 3. This invocation is done in the initialization section of the constructor as shown in the following syntax:

" *DerivedClass(argument list) : InitializationSection*

```
{
//Body of the constructor of the derived class
}"
```

The example code for this kind of invocation is used in the above example to invoke the constructor of the base class with the parameter a:

```
"D(int a) : B(a)
{
cout << "One-argument constrctor of the Derived Class is invoked";
}"
```

The following program illustrates how the parameterized constructors are invoked in both base class and derived class while object creation:

```
#include <iostream.h>
class B{
protected:
int x, y;
public:
B(int a, int b) : x(a), y(b) { } //x=a, y=b
};
class D : public B
{
int a, b;
public:
D(int p, int q, int r, int s) : B(p, q), a(r), b(s) { }
void Output()
{
cout<<"x = "<<x<<endl;
cout<<"y = "<<y<<endl;
cout<<"a = "<<a<<endl;
cout<<"b = "<<b<<endl;
}
};
void main()
{
D objD(5, 10, 15, 20);
objD.Output();
}
```

In this example, we have two classes B and D. B is a base class with only one constructor, which takes two parameters a and b, to assign its local variables x and y. D is a derived class, which also has one constructor that takes four parameters p, q, r and s namely.

The first two parameters p and q are for passing the values to the base class members and the other two (r and s) are used in initializing the local members of the derived class itself. The code for initialization in the constructor are written in the initialization section for both assigning the local members and to invoke the base class constructor for initializing its local members.

CHAPTER TWELVE

Virtual and Pure Virtual Functions

Virtual functions are member functions defined in a class, with the keyword virtual. Virtual functions allow derived class to redefine the member functions inherited from its base class. When a virtual function is redefined in a derived class, it will have the same function signature (same name, parameters and return type) but different body (different code). Such functions are called as Overridden functions.

The combination of these two elements – virtual and overridden functions, allows a programmer to define a function in both parent and derived class, but with different functionality (code). When a function is overridden in a derived class, the selection of the function from the appropriate class (parent or derived) is determined at run-time. This is known as Run-time Polymorphism.

To implement run-time polymorphism, we need an object pointer, a parent class having one or more virtual functions and a derived class with overridden member functions. The following is an example program for implementing run-time polymorphism:

```
class Base {
public:
virtual void display(void){
cout << "I am Object A \n";
}
};
class Derived : public Base {
public:
void display(void){
cout << "I am object B \n";
}
};
int main( ){
Base A;
Derived B;
Base *p = &A;
p-->display();
p = &B;
p-->display();
}
```

In this example, we have two classes: Base and Derived. The class Base is the parent class and class Derived is a derived class. Both the classes are having the same member function display(). The function display() is a virtual function in the base class, whereas it is overridden in the derived class. To make use of such functions effectively, we need an object pointer.

Use of Object Pointer:

An object pointer is a pointer of type class. If the object pointer is of type base class, it is known as base class pointer, where as derived class pointer is a pointer of type derived class. A base class pointer can be used for pointing both base class objects as well as derived class object. But a derived class pointer can point only the derived class object.

Using the base pointer, we can access both the virtual function defined in the base class as well as the overridden member function of the derived class. The selection of such functions through object pointer is determined based on the type of object, pointed by the pointer at the time of function call. When the base class pointer points a base object, the function call will invoke the base class version of the member function; if it pointes a derived class object, then the overridden function of the derived class will be called.

In function *main()* of the above example, we have two objects (A and B) and one object pointer p, which is derived from the base class Base. Object A is an object of type Base (i.e., base class object), and object B is of type Derived (i.e., derived class object).

At first, the pointer p is assigned with the address of the base class object A. And, using pointer p the function *display()* is called. This call will invoke the virtual member function of the base class, because the pointer points at the base class object A.

Then, the pointer p is assigned with the address of the derived class object B, and through p the function *display()* is called again. During this time, instead of calling the base class version of *display()*, the derived class version of *display()* is called due to the fact that the pointer p points at the derived class object. This is how run-time polymorphism works.

Pure Virtual function and Abstract Class:

When a virtual function is defined with out its body (null-body), it becomes a pure virtual function. A pure virtual function serves as a framework for future design of the class hierarchy. Pure virtual function can be declared just like a virtual function, but with the symbol "= 0" at the end of its definition as shows below:

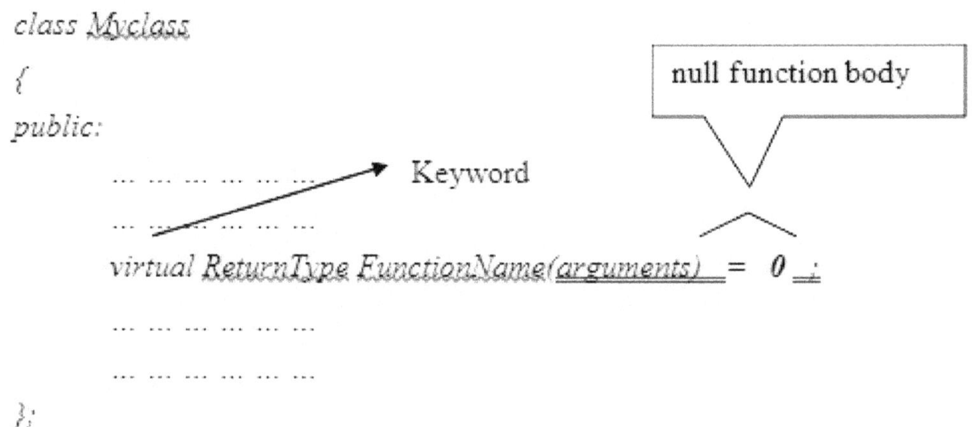

Fig. 12.1: Structure of a Pure Virtual Function

A pure virtual function has no implementation part in its base class. The implementation (body containing code) must be provided in a class, which is derived from the base class containing pure virtual function. Hence, a pure virtual function is an unfinished placeholder that the derived class is expected to complete. The following are the properties of pure virtual functions:

1. A pure virtual function has no implementation in the base class. Hence, a class with pure virtual function can't be instantiated.
2. It acts as a empty bucket that the derived class is supposed to fill.
3. A pure virtual member function can be invoked by its derived class.

The class containing one or more pure virtual function is called an Abstract base class, because the implementation part of one or more virtual functions are abstracted or separated from their function declaration. Abstract classes (classes with at least one virtual function) can be used as a framework upon which new classes can be built to provide new functionality.

Dynamic Memory Allocation

Dynamic allocation is nothing but knowing certain details which are required for memory allocation of variables during run-time. An example for dynamic allocation is dynamic array. For a dynamic array, the dimension of the array is determined only during run-time. But for a static array, the dimension of the array is specified in the code before compilation as follows:

```
float a[10];
```

The code required for creating a dynamic array is as follows:

```
float *a;
int n;
cin >> n;
a = new float[n];
```

In this example, the dimension of the array is obtained from the user and is stored in the variable n. Then using n, a new array is created dynamically and its starting address is assigned to the pointer variable a. Now, through this object pointer a, which points a floating array, we can access all the elements of the array.

Memory can be allocated to any type of variable, which includes simple variable, array variables or object variables. The following is an example for allocating memory dynamically for an object variable:

```
class X {
public:
int data;
};
main()
{
X *p = new X;
(*p).data = 22;
cout << (*p).data;
p-->data = 44;
cout << p-->data;
}
```

In the above example, memory is allocated dynamically for the object of class X, and the reference to the object is stored in the object pointer p. Then, the data member of object X is accessed through the pointer p using pointer operator (*) and indirection operator (-->) to manipulate the values 22 and 44.

The major difference between static and dynamic allocation is that the memory is allocated in heap storage for dynamic variables, whereas stack is used for static variables. The following is an example for creating a Student object dynamically through pointers:

```
#include <iostream.h>
#include <string.h>
#include <conio.h>
```

```
class Student
{
long int roll_no;
char *name;
public:
void SetData(long int prno, char *pname)
{
roll_no = prno;
name = pname;
}
void OutData();
};
void Student::OutData()
{
cout << "The Students details are ..." <endl;
cout << "Roll Number" << endl;
cout << "Name : " << name;
}
void main()
{
long int rno;
char sname[25];
Student *s;
s = new Student;
clrscr();
cout << "Enter the Roll-No. & Name of a Student :";
cin >> rno >> sname;
s-->SetData(rno, sname);
s-->OutData();
}
```

In the above program, function main() creates an object of class Student, which is defined with two data members and two member functions. The object creation is done at run time through an object pointer, i.e., the space for the new object is allocated only at run time based on the members defined in the class. Once the object is created, the reference to the object is return as a pointer, which can be stored in an object pointer for accessing its members.

A Vector Program:

The following is a C++ program that defines and creates a Vector object dynamically.

```
#include <iostream.h>
class Vector
{
int *v;
int sz;
Public:
Vector(int size)
{
sz = size;
v = new int[size];
```

```
}
Vector()
{
sz = 100;
v = new int[100];
}
void Read();
void Show_Sum();
~Vector()
{
delete v;
}
};
void Vector::Read()
{
for(int i = 0; i<sz; i++)
{
cout<<"Enter the element Vector["<<i<<"]?";
cin>>v[i];
}
}
void Vector::Show_Sum()
{
int sum = 0;
for(int i = 0; i<sz; i++)
sum += v[i];
cout << "Vector Sum is :"<<sum;
}
void main()
{
Vector *v1;
int count;
cout<<"Enter the Dimension of the Vector";
cin>>count;
set v1 = new Vector(count);
v1-->Read();
v1-->Show_Sum();
}
```

In function *main()*, the dimension of the vector is obtained during run time from the user. The vector is created dynamically in any one of the two constructors (default or parameterized constructor) and manipulated in *read()* and *show_sum()* member functions. After the execution of function *main()*, the vector v1 (vector pointed by v1) goes out of scope. This will invoke the destructor, which will deallocate the array dynamically allocated for the vector.

www.ingramcontent.com/pod-product-compliance
Ingram Content Group UK Ltd.
Pitfield, Milton Keynes, MK11 3LW, UK
UKHW061706190726
13853UKWH00008B/2427